NAZIM HIKMET
The Epic of Sheik Bedreddin

NAZIM HIKMET

The Epic of Sheik Bedreddin

and other poems

Translated by Randy Blasing and Mutlu Konuk

PERSEA BOOKS
New York

Some of these translations originally appeared in *The American Poetry Review, The Denver Quarterly, Persea,* and *A Review.*

Copyright ©1977 by Randy Blasing and Mutlu Konuk
All rights reserved.
For information, address the publisher:
Persea Books, Inc.
P.O. Box 804, Madison Square Station
New York, N.Y. 10010
International Standard Book Number: 0-89255-023-6, cloth
                                   0-89255-024-4, paper

Library of Congress Catalog Card Number: 77-76663
First Edition
Printed in the United States of America

CONTENTS

INTRODUCTION

NAZIM HIKMET, the first modern Turkish poet, is recognized around the world as one of the great international poets of the twentieth century. His poetry has been translated into more than fifty languages, yet he is still not widely known in the United States. Born in 1902 and raised in Istanbul, Hikmet left Allied-occupied Turkey after the First World War and ended up in Moscow, where he attended the university and met writers and artists from all over the world. He returned to Turkey after the Turkish Independence, was subsequently arrested for working on a leftist magazine, and managed to escape to Russia, where he continued to write plays and poems. In 1928 a general amnesty allowed Hikmet to return to Turkey, and during the next ten years he published nine books of poetry — five collections and four long poems — while working as a proofreader, journalist, scriptwriter, and translator. At the same time, he was constantly harassed by the Turkish secret police and served a number of short prison sentences totaling almost four years. Then in January 1938 he was arrested and charged with inciting the army to revolt; on the evidence that military cadets were found reading his poems, he was sentenced to twenty-eight years.

In prison Hikmet continued writing; between 1941 and 1945, for instance, he completed the epic *Human Landscapes from My Country*, parts of which were lost or destroyed in being smuggled out of prison and which now runs about 17,000 lines. In 1949 a world-wide committee of writers, artists, and intellectuals — including Neruda, Picasso, and Sartre — was founded in Paris and began compaigning for his release, and in 1950 Hikmet went on an eighteen-day hunger strike, despite just having suffered a heart attack. He won the World Peace Prize the same year and eventually was freed in a general amnesty in 1950. Less than a year later, however, Hikmet was forced to leave his family behind and flee Turkey to escape being drafted — at forty-eight — by the Turkish army. During his exile he lived in Russia but traveled widely and continued to be productive until his death in Moscow in June 1963.

It was only after Hikmet's death that his books began to appear again in Turkey; in 1965-66, for example, more than twenty books by Hikmet were published there, some of them reprints of earlier books and others works appearing for the first time. Since then, numerous selections of his poems have come out, as have all five volumes of *Human Landscapes*. At the same time, several biographies of Hikmet have been published, and his novels, plays, letters, and even children's stories have also been published. His *Collected Works* started appearing in 1975, and today Hikmet is generally recognized in Turkey as one of the best poets ever to write in Turkish.

In preparing our second selection of Hikmet's poetry we have chosen poems that together present the unfolding drama of his life and the parallel development of his work. For in the course of his forty-year career his poetry changed considerably as he wrote in response to his experience — both his personal experience and the greater history of the thirties, the Second World War, and its aftermath. His poems and his experience stand in a complex, dynamic relationship to each other, and if his poetry got him into trouble — "The Epic of Sheik Bedreddin," for example, landed him in prison — it also gave him the will and the means to withstand imprisonment and even exile.

In this selection, then, we see Hikmet start out in the twenties as the young revolutionary poet of the deft, irreverent, and tough early poems and change into the accomplished, historically and politically aware poet of the masterly "Epic of Sheik Bedreddin." Published in 1936, this "epic" is based on an early fifteenth-century peasants' uprising against the Ottoman Empire. Sheik Bedreddin, the Turkish mystic and great Islamic scholar, translated his belief in the immanence of God into political action and advocated a kind of social-ism, which declared the oneness of all people and religions and called for the abolition of private property. The uprising that Bedreddin inspired was led in western Turkey by two of his disciples, Börklüje Mustafa and Torlak Kemal. The poem is primarily about this event — the joint rebellion of Turkish, Greek, and Jewish peasants who seized the lands of the feudal lords, worked them together, and together defended them until their bloody defeat by the Sultan's army. The form of the poem does justice to its historical subject. Both the history of Bedreddin's rebellion and the actuality of Hik-met's daily life in prison are transformed into a kind of poetry that itself embodies a historical necessity. Not only is the course of events a necessary sequence, but their very telling has the temporal necessity of a piece of music; every line — every word — has to be as and where it is. Thus Hikmet achieves a sense of formal necessity without formal regularity, and the poem becomes totally compelling.

While the discoveries of "The Epic of Sheik Bedreddin" led to the writing of *Human Landscapes* after Hikmet's final imprisonment in 1938, the shorter poems of the prison years have yet another voice. In these poems we hear a vulnerable but hopeful, realistic yet lyrical, fully *human* poet. The se-quence "9-10 P.M. Poems," which Hikmet wrote for his wife at night while working on *Human Landscapes* during the day, pieces together a whole consciousness, whose personal drama unfolds as part of a larger history. These love poems escape being simply personal because Hikmet's love for his wife is in-separable from his love for his city, and his yearning for both is inseparable from his hope for better days for people every-where. Set against the background of the end of the Second World War, the coming of winter, and his continuing im-prisonment, these taut, lucid poems embody the special ur-gency of a faith based on will.

After years of being confined in prisons, Hikmet travels freely during his exile, and the poems from this period reflect

9

the speeding-up of his experience. Not only the speed of his travels through space in trains and planes but his sense, as he nears death, of an acceleration of time underlies the breathless rhythms of a late poem like "Straw-Blond," where the almost-monotonous pace of run-on perceptions is not broken even by punctuation. "Straw-Blond," which comes out of Hikmet's experience of a suddenly expanded universe, answers the needs that such experience creates, for the poem that travels freely in time and space at breakneck speed ends not in chaotic dispersion but in the formal and human unity of its closing lines. And in the discovery of this larger vision of wholeness Hikmet's poetry and his life play out the final act to enable him to live with the fact of exile and the idea of death.

Mutlu Konuk

NAZIM HIKMET
The Epic of Sheik Bedreddin

THE POET'S MOMENTARY LAZINESS

The sunny blue flowing broadside
      slowed to a stop.
The bridge sounded the bell,
      the capstan unwound,
sleep anchored in my eyes.

Misty riders
        on misty horses
ambushed
        the red corpuscles in my blood,
taps blew
      in my brain.
The pencil in my hand
          grew
             long
                and thick
and took the shape of a broomstick;
my hand became an old streetsweeper,
      leaned on its broom,
          and slept!!!
S-
  sl-
    sleee. . .

Colors on the shoulders of sounds,
lights on the laps of shadows —
        they flow. . .

In my brain's command book there's only one **command**:
Do nothing!!!
      Motionless
        unmoving
sit empty like an empty barrel. . .

Nothing
    nothing at all. . .
No love, no hate, no pity, no malice, no nothing. . .

But suddenly
a second Japan broke up in my stomach!
Hunger
    thumbed its nose double
                and stuck out its tongue.

Death
waved its yellow hanky
           like a bony cackle. . .
I sat up. . .
The sleep in my eyes
          weighed anchor.
The misty riders
      dissolved.
The commander who wrote in my brain's command book
    fled from his tent in disgrace.
The old streetsweeper grabbed his broom —
grabbed it and
      put it back
in the service of those who sweep
          the evils of the globe.

1923

THE WORM IN MY BODY

You
entered
the towering pine of my body
like a soft
white
worm
and you ate.
Like an English worker feeding the worm MacDonald
in his intestines, I carry you
            inside me.

But I know
            who's to blame!

Woman, your soul is a House of Lords!
You're a hairless Poincaré in skirts!
To burn
before me
like a red-hot locomotive engine
is an easy trick for you.
Another thing you're good at
is wriggling like skates on ice!
Cold!
Hot!
Harlot!
Stop!
Soft
        and white
        you're twisting
                into my brain
                    and you're eating!
You can't go in there!
You can't eat that!

I yanked out
like a rotten tooth
the soft
white worm
twisting into my brain!
I sweated a lot!
This was the last
            this won't happen again.

1924

ON THE EVE OF A HOLIDAY

If not tonight
then tomorrow
            night
I'll be thrown in prison.

Not a leaf moves inside me.
Inside me, boundless
                    peace
                            like sound sleep.

Boundless
            peace
                    inside —
from watching
the blues
            in the air like a new-
                        born child. . .

Yesterday
I
went to the city square:
"Let's not kill
            our brothers for them,"
                                    I said.

And if not tonight
then tomorrow
night
        I'll be thrown in prison. . .

Not a leaf moves inside me. . .
I put my hands under my head. . .

I hear the sea. . .
    I sleep. . .

June 1930

ON SHIRTS, TROUSERS, CAPS, AND FELT HATS

If there are those
who would call
   me
     "the enemy
       of a clean shirt,"
they should see a picture of my great teacher.
The master of masters, Marx,
     had his jacket in pawn,
and maybe he ate one meal every four days;
but
  his awesome beard
  flowed down
   over a snow-white,
    spotless,
  starched shirt. . .
And who gave the death sentence to pressed trousers?
Smart guys
   should read our history here too:
"In 1848, as bullets parted his hair,
  he would wear
   trousers of genuine English material,
    in true English style,
   pressed and waxed
   à l'anglaise —
   the greatest of men, Engels. . .
When Vladimir Ilyich Ulyanov Lenin
appeared at the barricades like a fiery giant,
he had on a collar
    and a tie too. . ."
As for me,
me who's just another proletarian poet —
Marxist-Leninist consciousness,
   30 kilos of bones,

7 liters of blood,
about a couple kilometers
of blood vessels,
muscles, flesh, skin, and nerves —
the cap on my head
doesn't tell
what's inside it,
any more than my only felt hat
makes me a tool
of the past that is passing. . .
Yet if I
wear a cap
six days a week,
it's so that one day a week
when I'm out with my girl
I can wear
clean
my only felt hat. . .
But why
don't I have two felt hats?
What do you say, master?
Am I lazy?
No!
To bind pages
12 hours a day,
to stand on my feet
till I'm dead,
is to work to the hilt. . .
Are we abysmally ignorant?
No!
For instance,
it wouldn't seem
I'm as backward
as Mr. "Sat-Sin". . .
Am I foolish?

Well,
        not
                too much. . .
Maybe a little sloppy. . .
But all the time
        the real reason:
                I'm a proletarian,
                        brother,
                                a proletarian!!
And I will own two felt hats
        — two million felt hats —
only if,
like every
                proletarian,
I own — we own —
        the textile mills
        of Barcelona-Habik-Mosan-Manchester!. . .
And if n-o-o-o-o-t,
        NOT!!!

                                5 February 1931

AMNESTY

I put down the thousand-and-one-nights book.
I lit a cigarette.
I looked
      out through the bars:
each star
      gleamed
           like a magic mirror.
Night.
Bursa Prison.
The waters
of a god-forsaken
black lake
      stirred.
Excitement
      the length
          of "Murder One," first floor;
the pointed black
      hats
        are excited.
Lips white,
      brows knitted.
A drop of light
      oozed from a crack in the wall.
The city of the blind
      goes forward, muttering.
The blind
      head for the dream in their darkness!
"Amnesty!"
      they say,
"we'll get out,
wear our hats
cocked.
Earth,

sun,
women,
air. . .
Ride a boat, ride a train,
take a trolley!
No cuffs,
no cops —
on our own,
all alone,
knock about,
get around!
Sleep in a forest, cross a mountain!
Go around all you want!"

The pointed black hats are excited!

Prison is impossible without dreaming. . .
Yet I. . .
I look and here my cigarette's burned out in my hand —
I never took a puff.

10/22/1933

LETTER TO MY WIFE

11-11-33
Bursa
Prison

My only one!
In your last letter you say:
"My head is throbbing,
          my heart is stunned!"
You say:
"If they hang you,
       if I lose you,
             I can't live!"
You can live, my dear,
my memory will vanish like black smoke in the wind.
Of course you'll live, red-haired lady of my heart:
in the twentieth century,
              grief lasts
                    a year at most.
Death —
a body swinging from a rope.
My heart just
          doesn't accept this death.
But
you can be sure of this:
          if some poor gypsy's hairy black
                  spidery hand
                        is going to slip the rope
                              around my neck,
they'll look in vain to see fear
                    in the blue eyes
                          of Nazim!

I,
in the twilight of my last morning,
will see my friends and you,
and I'll take
to the earth
            only the pain of an unfinished song. . .

My wife!
Good-hearted,
golden,
eyes sweeter than honey — my bee!
Why did I write you
            they want to hang me?
The trial has only begun,
and they don't just pluck a man's head
            like a turnip.
Look, forget all this.
This is all farfetched.
If you have any money,
            buy me some flannel underwear:
my sciatica is acting up again.
And don't forget,
the wife of a prisoner
            must always think good things.

THE EPIC OF SHEIK BEDREDDIN

I was reading "The Simavne Governor's Son Bedreddin," a treatise written by Mehmet Sherefeddin Effendi, Professor of Scripture at the University's School of Theology, and printed in the year 1341 (1925) by the Evkafi Islamiye. I had come to the sixty-fifth page of the treatise. On the sixty-fifth page of this professor of scripture, Ducas — who was serving the Genoese as confidential secretary — was saying:

> At that time, a common Turkish peasant appeared in the mountainous country situated at the entrance to the Bay of Ionia and designated as Stylarium-Karaburun in the language of the people. Stylarium is situated across from the island of Chios. The said peasant was preaching and giving counsel to the Turks and advising that, with the exception of women, the whole of things such as food, clothing, livestock, and land should be considered the joint property of all the people.

The confidential secretary to the Genoese, who explained so simply and so clearly the counsel and advice of the common Turkish peasant in Stylarium, passed before me with his black velvet robe, pointed beard, and long, sallow, ceremonious face. That Börklüje Mustafa, the greatest disciple of the Simavne governor's son Bedreddin, should be called "common" made me smile — at both senses of the word. Then suddenly I thought of the author of the treatise, Mehmet Sherefeddin Effendi. This professor of scripture who wrote,

> That Börklüje Mustafa, who was advising that such things as foodstuffs, livestock, and land should be considered joint public property, should except

women from this seems to us to be an evasion and a deception that he chose to practice in the face of public opinion. For it is certain that his sheik, who believed in the oneness of creation, did not give specific instructions to Mustafa to make this exception . . . ,

was, I found, so well versed in geomancy that he could divine in the earth cast over the centuries the innermost thoughts of people. And I thought of two sentences from Marx and Engels:

The bourgeois sees in his wife a mere means of production. When he hears that the means of production are to be socialized, he naturally can come to no other conclusion than that this socialization will extend to women as well.

Why shouldn't the professor of the University's School of Theology think about Bedreddin's medieval peasant socialism what the bourgeois thinks about modern industrial socialism? From the point of view of theology, aren't women property?

I closed the book. My eyes burned, but I wasn't sleepy. I looked at the Chemin de Fer watch hanging on a nail over my bed. Almost two. A cigarette. Another cigarette. I listen to the sounds circulating in the hot, still air of the prison ward, which smells heavy like stagnant water. The ward, with its sweating cement and twenty-eight people besides me, is asleep. The guards in the towers sounded their whistles again, they're more frequent and more piercing tonight. Whenever the whistles go wild with a mad contagion like this — possibly for no reason at all — I think I'm on a ship sinking in the dark night.

From the ward above us came the rattle of the chained

bandits condemned to death. Their papers are in the appeals court. Ever since that rainy night they returned with their sentences, they pace like this, clanking their chains until morning.

When we're taken out to the back yard during the day, how many times I've looked up at their windows. Three people. Two sit in the window on the right, one in the window on the left. They say the one who was caught first and turned in his friends is the one who sits by himself. He's also the one who smokes the most cigarettes.

All three of them wrap their arms around the iron bars. Although they can see the sea and the mountains very well from where they are, they only look down, at the yard, at us, at people.

I've never heard their voices. In the entire prison they are the only ones who never sing — not even once. And if their chains, which speak like this only at night, suddenly fall silent very early one morning, the prison will know that in the most crowded square of the city hang three long white shirts, their chests labeled.

If I just had an aspirin. My palms burn. My head is full of Bedreddin and Börklüje Mustafa. If I could push myself to go a little further, if my head didn't ache so much that my eyes blur, I would be able to see — among the clattering swords, neighing horses, cracking whips, and crying women and children of distant years — the faces of Bedreddin and Mustafa like two bright words of hope.

My eyes fell on the book I'd just put down on the cement. It has a purplish cover the color of sour cherries, half of it faded from the sun. On the cover, the title of the treatise is written in Arabic script like a sultan's monogram. The torn edges of the yellowed pages stick out from under the cover. I think: Bedreddin must be saved from the Arabic script, antique pen-case, reed pen, and blotting powder of this professor of theology. In my head there are lines from Arabshah, Ashikpashazade, Neshri, Idris of Bitlis, Ducas, and even Sherefeddin Effendi — lines I have read over and over until I know them by heart:

There is a strong possibility that the date of Bedreddin's birth would have to be placed at around 770.

Bedreddin, who completed his education in Egypt, remained there many years and doubtless attained great learning in this milieu.

Upon his return to Edirne from Egypt, he found his parents still living.

While his arrival here could have been for the purpose of visiting his mother and father, the possibility also exists that he might have come on the invitation of Prince Musa, who had jurisdiction over this city.

When Sultan Mehmet I came to power by defeating his brothers, he assigned Sheik Bedreddin to reside in Iznik.

In the preface to the *Foundations*, which he completed here, the Sheik wrote, "The fire in my heart has burst into flame. And it's mounting daily, so that were my heart hard as iron, it would melt."

When they banished the Sheik to Iznik, his chief disciple Börklüje Mustafa removed to Aydin. He made his way from there to Karaburun.

He was saying, "As I could have the use of your possessions, you could in the same way have the use of my possessions." After he had won the common peasants to his side with such sayings, he tried to establish friendship with the Christians. Although Sultan Mehmet's Saruhan governor Sisman moved against this false prophet, he was unable to penetrate the narrow passes of Stylarium.

When the Simavne governor's son Bedreddin heard how the situation of Börklüje was progressing, he fled Iznik. He arrived in Sinope. Eventually he boarded a ship and landed in the province of Walachia. From there he fled to the Mad Forest in Dobruja.

At this time, word of the intrigues and heresies of the agitator Mustafa, the designated representative of the aforesaid Bedreddin in the province of Aydin, reached Sultan Mehmet's ear. Immediately an imperial edict was handed down to Prince Murad, ruler of Amasya and Little Rumelia, that he set out to remove the heretic Mustafa by assembling a regiment of Anatolian soldiers and that he descend on Mustafa in the province of Aydin with a full complement of men and equipment.

Mustafa, with a force of nearly ten thousand of his seditious and subversive followers, stood up to defy the Prince.

A great battle took place.

After much blood was spilt, with divine guidance the godless forces were defeated.

The survivors were brought to Seljuk. Even the most terrible tortures applied to Mustafa could not turn him from his obsession. Mustafa was stretched on a cross on a camel. After his hands were nailed to the wood, he was led through the city in a great procession. His confidants who remained loyal to him were killed before his eyes. Shouting "Come, Grand Sultan Mustafa!" they gave up their souls and died at peace.

Lastly they tore Börklüje Mustafa to pieces and inspected the ten provinces; satisfied, they granted fiefs to the soldiers. Bayezid Pasha returned to Manisa and found there Bedreddin's disciple Torlak Kemal. And there he hanged him.

At this time, the situation of Bedreddin in Dobruja was improving. People came from everywhere and gathered around him. He was very close to uniting all the people. For this reason, the personal intervention of Sultan Mehmet became necessary.

On the suggestion of Bayezid Pasha, certain persons infiltrated the professional followers and disciples of Bedreddin. And taking the proper precautions, they arrested Bedreddin in the forest and bound him up.

They brought him to Sultan Mehmet in Serrai. Accompanying Sultan Mehmet was an advisor named Mevlana Haydar who had newly arrived from Persia. Mevlana Haydar stated: "According to Islamic law, the killing of this man is holy, but his substance is unholy."

From there they carried the Simavne governor's son Bedreddin to the market place and hanged him in front of a shop. After some days, a few of his unclean disciples appeared and took him away. Even today he has disciples in that region.

My head is splitting. I checked my watch. It's stopped. The rattle of chains upstairs has let up. Only one of them is still pacing. He must be the one who sits alone in the window on the left.

I have to hear an Anatolian song. It seems to me that if the highwaymen started singing that mountain song again, my headache would disappear on the spot.

I lit another cigarette. I reached down and picked Mehmet Sherefeddin Effendi's treatise up from the cement. A wind has come up outside. It's grumbling under the window, shutting out the sounds of the sea, chains, and whistles. It must be rocky below the window. How many times we've tried to look down there where our wall meets the sea. But it's impossible. The iron bars of the window are too close together. You can't stick your head out. So here we see the sea only as a horizon.

Next to my bed was the lathe-turner Shefik's bed. Shefik rolled over in his sleep, mumbling something. The wedding quilt his wife sent him slipped off. I covered him up.

I turned again to the sixty-fifth page of the professor of scripture of the School of Theology. I had read only a couple of lines from the First Secretary to the Genoese when I heard a voice through the pain in my head.

The voice said: "Silently I passed the waves of the sea to be here with you."

I turned around. Someone's at the window. That's who is speaking.

"Have you forgotten what Ducas, First Secretary to the Genoese, wrote? Don't you remember his speaking of a Cretan monk who lived on Chios in a monastery called

Turlut? I, 'one of Börklüje Mustafa's dervishes,' didn't I used to visit that monk like this over the waves of the sea, bareheaded, barefoot, wrapped in a piece of cloth?"

I looked at the one who spoke these words standing big as life outside the bars where there wasn't anything for him to hold on to. He really was as he said. His seamless robe flowed down white.

Now, years later, as I write these lines, I think of the theology professor. I don't know if Sherefeddin Effendi is dead or alive. But if he's alive and reads what I write, he'll say: "What a fake! He claims to be a materialist and then, like the Cretan monk, goes on — and centuries after the event! — about talking with Mustafa's disciple who silently crosses seas."

And I can almost hear the divine laughter with which the master of scripture will follow these words.

But no matter. Let his excellency laugh. And I'll tell my story.

My headache was suddenly gone. I got out of bed. I walked up to the one in the window. He took me by the hand. We left the sleeping ward with its sweating cement and its twenty-eight people besides me. Suddenly I found myself where we could never see — on the rocks where our wall meets the sea. Side by side, Mustafa's disciple and I passed over the waves of the dark sea and went behind the years, centuries back, to the time of Sultan Mehmet I.

This journey is the adventure I want to tell you about. And the spectacle of sounds, colors, movements, and shapes that I saw on this journey I'll try to capture piece by piece and mostly — according to an old habit — in assorted long and short lines with an occasional rhyme. Like this:

1.

On the divan Bursa silk in green-branching red boughs,
a blue garden of Kütahya tiles on the wall,
wine in silver pitchers,
in copper pots lambs roasted golden brown.
Strangling his own brother Musa with a bowstring
— purified with his brother's blood in a gold bowl —
Sultan Mehmet had ascended the throne and was sovereign.
Mehmet was sovereign but
in the land of Osman
the wind was a barren cry, a death-song.
The peasant's work done by the light of his eyes
and by the sweat of his brow
                              was a fief.
The cracked water jugs were dry,
at the springs there were horsemen twisting their mustaches.
On the roads, a traveler could hear the wail of men without land
                              and land without men.
And as foaming horses neighed and swords clashed
              at the door of the castle at the end of the roads,
the market place was in disorder,
              the guilds had lost faith in their masters.
In short, there was a sovereign, a fief, a wind, a wail.

2.
This is Iznik Lake.
It is still.
Dark.

Deep.
It's like a well
    in the mountains.

Around here lakes
are smoky.
    Their fish taste flat,
    their marshes breed malaria,
    and the men die before white shows in their beards.

This is Iznik Lake.
Next to it, the town of Iznik.
In the town of Iznik,
the blacksmith's anvil is a broken heart.
The children are hungry.
The women's breasts are like dried fish.
And the young men don't sing.

This is the town of Iznik.
This is a house
in the workers' quarter.
In this house
there's an old man named Bedreddin.
Small build,
    big beard —
        white.
Sly, slanting, child's eyes,
and yellow fingers like reeds.

Bedreddin
is sitting
on a white sheepskin.
In Persian script he's writing
        the *Foundations.*
They are on their knees, facing him.
And at a distance,

as if looking at a mountain, they look at him.
He looks:
head shaved,
eyebrows bushy,
tall and rangy Börklüje Mustafa.
He looks:
hawk-nosed Torlak Kemal.
They don't tire of looking,
they cannot look enough,
they're looking at the Iznik exile Bedreddin.

3.
On the shore a barefoot woman is crying.
And in the lake
      an empty fishing boat has broken loose
      and floats on the water
      like a dead bird.
It goes where the water takes it,
across the lake to be smashed on the mountains.

Evening came to Iznik Lake.
Thick-voiced horsemen in the mountains
slit the sun's throat
      and drained the blood into the lake.
On the shore a barefoot woman is crying,
the wife of the fisherman chained in the castle
               for taking a carp.

Evening came to Iznik Lake.
Bedreddin knelt down,
      cupped water in his hands, and stood up.
And as the water
slipped through his fingers
and returned to the lake,
         he said to himself:

"The fire in my heart
has burst into flame
and is mounting daily.
Were my heart wrought iron, it could not resist this,
it would melt . . .
I will come out now and declare myself! [1]
Men of the land, we will conquer the land.
And realizing the power of knowledge and the mystery
of Oneness,
we shall abolish the laws of nations and religions . . ."

*

The next day,
as the boat was smashed in the lake,
a head was cut off in the castle,
a woman cried on the shore,

and as the one from Simavne
wrote his *Foundations*,
Torlak Kemal and Mustafa
kissed
their sheik's hand.
They saddled their roan horses
and rode out through the gates of Iznik,
each with a naked sword at his sid
and a handwritten book in his saddlebag.

The book:
Bedreddin's *Illuminations*.

4.

After Börklüje Mustafa and Torlak Kemal took

---

1. "I will come out now and declare myself, that with my believers I may come into possession of the world. And with the power of knowledge and the revelation of the mystery of Oneness, we shall abolish the pretenders' laws and religions" — the Sheik's words as reported by the author of *Eight Heavens* in M.S.'s translation.

37

their leave of Bedreddin and mounted their horses
and rode off, one for Aydin and the other for Manisa,
I left with my guide for Konya, and one day, upon
reaching the Haymana plain,

We heard Mustafa had appeared
in Karaburun in Aydin.
He spoke Bedreddin's word
in the audience of peasants.

We heard: "That the people might be freed of their suffering
and the earth's flesh be made pure
                as the skin of a fifteen-year-old boy,
the landowners have been slaughtered wholesale
and the lords' fiefs made public land."

We heard . . .
Can one hear of such things and sit still?
Early one morning,
as a lone bird sang on the Haymana plain,
we ate olives under a scrawny willow.
"Let's go,
            we said,
and see.
Grab
        a plow,
and let's us work this brother's land
                            for a stretch,
                            we said."

We hit the mountains,
and left mountains behind . . .

Friends,
I don't travel alone.
One afternoon I said to my companion:

We're here.
I said: Look.
The earth that wept just a step back
started to laugh like a child before our eyes.
Look, the figs are like big emeralds,
the vines can barely hold the amber clusters.
See the fish jumping in the reed baskets:
their sparkling wet skin shimmers,
and their meat is white and tender
                    like a young lamb's.
I said: Look,
here man is fertile like the earth, sun, and sea,
here the sea, sun, and earth bear fruit like man.

5.

When we left the fiefdoms of the sovereign and his lords behind and crossed into Börklüje Mustafa's country, we were met first by three young men. All three wore seamless white robes like my guide. One had a curly, ebony-black beard, passionate eyes the same color, and a big hooked nose. He used to be of Moses's faith. Now he was one of Mustafa's braves.

The second one had a pointed chin and a straight nose. He was a Greek sailor from Chios. He too was a disciple of Mustafa.

The third was of medium height and broad-shouldered. When I think of him now, I liken him to Hüseyin who sings that mountain song in the highwaymen's ward. Except Hüseyin comes from Erzurum. This one was from Aydin.

The one from Aydin spoke first: "Are you friend or foe? If you are friends, welcome. If you are enemies, your next breath will be your last."

"We're friends," we said.

Upon which we learned that in the high passes of Karaburun they had just destroyed the army of the Saruhan governor Sisman, who tried to return the lands to their sovereign lords.

Again, the one who looked like Hüseyin said: "If, on our brother's table that stretches from here to the sea off Karaburun, the figs are so honeyed this year, the grain this heavy, and the olives so fat, it is because we watered them with the blood of the gilt-jacketed despoilers."

The joyful news was very great.

"Then let us return immediately, let us bear the tidings to Bedreddin," my guide said.

Taking with us Anastos, the sailor from Chios, we left the brothers' land we had barely set foot in, and plunged once more into the darkness of the sons of Osman.

We found Bedreddin in Iznik on the shore of the lake. It was morning. The air was damp and sad.

"Now it's our turn," Bedreddin said. "We'll leave for Rumelia."

We left Iznik at night. Horsemen pursued us. The darkness was like a wall between us and them. And we could hear their hoofbeats behind this wall. My guide led the way. Bedreddin's horse was between my roan horse and Anastos's. We three were like mothers, Bedreddin was our child. We were breathless for fear that they might do him harm. We were like three children, Bedreddin was our father. Whenever the hoofbeats behind the wall of darkness seemed to come nearer, we moved closer to Bedreddin.

Hiding in daylight and traveling by night, we reached Sinope. There we set sail.

6.
Stars and a sailboat alone

                on a sea one night.

On a sea one night a sailboat
                          alone with the stars.
The stars were without number.
The sails were down.
The water was dark
                  and flat as far as the eye could see.
Blond Anastos and the islander Bekir
                              were at the oars.
I was in the bow
              with Bull Salih.
And Bedreddin,
          his fingers buried in his beard,
                  was listening to the oars splash.

"Well, Bedreddin!"
      I said.
          "We see nothing but stars
                    above the sleeping sails.
No whispers stir the air.
And no sounds
              rise from the sea.
Only mute, dark water,
      only its sleep."
The little old man with the white beard bigger than himself
                                    laughed.
                          He said:
"Never mind about the stillness of the air,
the deep sleeps to awaken."

Stars and a sailboat alone
                      on a sea one night.
One night a boat sailed the Black Sea
                  headed for the Mad Forest,
                        the Sea of Trees . . .

7.
We landed in this forest, this Mad Forest,
we pitched our tents in the Sea of Trees.
We flew a falcon from every branch to every village
        with the message, "You know why we have come,
                you know the trouble in our heart."

Every falcon came back with a hundred lionhearts.
They all came — the peasant burning the master's crop,
                the apprentice the shop,
                        the serf leaving his chains.
All those like us in Rumelia came,
        an army flowing to the Sea of Trees.

What pandemonium!
A blur
        of horses, men, spears, iron, leaves,
        leather, beech branches, oak roots.
Since the Mad Forest went mad,
it hadn't seen such revelry
                or heard such a din . . .

8.
        Leaving Anastos in Bedreddin's camp in the Mad
Forest, my guide and I went down to Gallipoli. Some-
one long before us swam this strait — for love, I guess.
We too swam across to the other side. But what made
us quick as fish was not the desire to see a woman's
face in the moonlight but the need to reach Kara-
burun via Izmir with news — this time, for Mustafa
from his sheik.
        When we stopped at a caravanserai near Izmir, we
heard that Bayezid Pasha, who led the Sultan's twelve-
year-old son Murad by the hand, was gathering Ana-
tolian soldiers.
        We didn't waste time in Izmir. We had just left

the city by the Aydin road when we came upon four gentlemen in a vineyard resting and chatting under a walnut tree while they waited for the watermelons they'd lowered into a well to cool. Each one had a different costume; three wore turbans, one a fez. They greeted us, we greeted them back. One of the turbaned was Neshri the historian. He said: "Sultan Mehmet sends Bayezid Pasha against Börklüje Mustafa, who invites the people to a religion of libertinism."

The second turban was Shekerullah bin Shehabeddin. He said: "Numerous persons have gathered around this mystic. And many of their practices that are clearly contrary to Islamic law have come to light."

The third turbaned personage was the historian Ashikpashazade. He said: "Question: if the aforesaid Mustafa is torn to pieces, will he go with faith or without? Answer: God alone knows, for it is not given to us to know the final state of his soul."

The gentleman in the fez was the professor of scripture of the School of Theology. He looked at us. He blinked his eyes and gave us a sly smile. He didn't say a thing.

At that, we dug our spurs into our horses and left. Leaving behind in the dust of our hooves the gentlemen chatting under a walnut tree in a vineyard while cooling the watermelons they'd lowered into a well, we reached Karaburun and Börklüje Mustafa.

9.
It was hot.
Hot.
The heat
      was a dull knife dripping blood.

It was hot.

The clouds were full.
The clouds were about
                to burst.
Motionless, he looked:
                his eyes like two eagles dived
                        down from the rocks
                                into the plain.
There the softest, hardest,
most generous, thriftiest,
most
        loving,
biggest, most beautiful woman
                                EARTH
                        was about
                                to give birth.

It was hot.
He looked out from the Karaburun mountains.
Brows knitted, he looked at the horizon,
                        at the end of this earth:
plucking the heads of children in the meadows
like bloody poppies
and dragging the naked cries in its wake,
a five-star fire swept across the horizon.
It was
        Prince Murad.
An imperial edict had been handed down to Prince Murad
that he hasten to Aydin
and descend on Bedreddin's designated representative Mustafa.

It was hot.
Bedreddin's representative, heretic Mustafa, looked,
peasant Mustafa looked
without fear
                anger
                        or a smile.

He looked straight
                    ahead.
He looked.
The softest, hardest,
most generous, thriftiest,
most
        loving,
biggest, most beautiful woman
                              EARTH
                was about
                    to give birth.

He looked.
Bedreddin's braves looked out from the rocks at the horizon.
The end of this earth was coming closer
                on the wings of a decreed bird of death.
And yet they
                who looked out from the rocks
had opened up this earth
like a brother's table spread for all —
this earth with its
grapes, figs, pomegranates,
sheep with fleece blonder than honey
                and milk thicker than honey,
and thin-waisted, lion-maned horses.

It was hot.
He looked.
Bedreddin's braves looked out at the horizon . . .

It was hot.
The clouds were full.
The first drop was about to fall like a sweet word.
All
        of a sudden,

as if streaming down from the rocks
          raining down from the sky
                    and springing up from the ground,
Bedreddin's braves faced the Prince's army
like the last work of this earth.
With flowing white robes
          bare heads
                    bare feet and bare swords.

A great battle took place.

Turkish peasants from Aydin,
          Greek sailors from Chios,
                    Jewish craftsmen,
Börklüje Mustafa's ten thousand heretical comrades
plunged into the forest of enemies like ten thousand axes.

The ranks of green and red flags,
          inlaid shields,
                    and bronze helmets
were torn apart but,
as the day descended into night in pouring rain,
the ten thousand were two thousand.

That they might sing as one voice
and together pull the net from the water,
that they might all work iron like lace
and all together plow the earth,
that they might eat the honeyed figs together,
that they might say,
                    "Everywhere
                    all together
                              in everything
                              but the lover's cheek,"
the ten thousand gave eight thousand . . .

They were defeated.

The victors wiped their bloody swords
            on the flowing white robes
                    of the defeated.
And the earth that brothers worked all together
like a song sung together
was ripped up
                by the hooves of horses bred in the Edirne palace.
Don't say
      this is the necessary result
      of historical, social, and economic conditions —
                                I know!
My head bows before the thing you speak of.
But the heart
      doesn't understand this language too well.
It
says, "O fickle Fate —
O cruel Fate!"
And they pass one by one,
their shoulders slashed by whips,
                    faces bloody,
in a flash they pass,
their bare feet crushing my heart,
the defeated of Karaburun pass through Aydin . . . [1]

---

1. Now as I write these lines I think of certain young men who pass for
"leftists" and who'll be saying things like: "Well! He separates his head and his
heart; he says his head accepts the historical, social, and economic conditions,
but his heart still burns. Well, well — will you look at the Marxist!" The way I
thought of the professor of scripture and heard his laugh at the very beginning
of this work . . . .
      And if I am now making such a statement, it is not for these young men.
It is for those who are far beyond the leftist affectations of the recent discov-
erers of Marxism.
      If a doctor has a tubercular child, if the doctor knows that his child will
die, if he accepts this as a physiological, biological, I-don't-know-what-logical
necessity, and if the child dies, the doctor — who well knew the necessity of
this death — won't he shed a single tear for his child?
      Marx, who knew that the Paris Commune would be overthrown, who
knew the historical, social, and economic conditions necessitating its over-

10.

They stopped at dark.
It was he who spoke:
"The city of Seljuk has set up shop.
Now whose neck, friends,
            whose neck is it now?"

The rain
        kept on.
They spoke,
        they said to him:
"It isn't
        set up —
                it will be.
The wind hasn't
        stopped —
                it will.
His throat isn't
        cut —
                it will be."

As rain seeped into the folds of the darkness,
I appeared at their side,
I spoke and said:
"Where are the gates of the city of Seljuk?
            Show me so I can go!
Does it have a fortress?
Tell me and I'll raze it.
Is there a toll?
            Speak so I don't pay!"

---

throw, didn't he feel the great dead of the Commune pass through his heart like a "song of pain"? And wasn't there at least a touch of sadness in the voices of those who shouted, "The Commune is dead, long live the Commune"?

A Marxist is not a "mechanical man" — a ROBOT; he is, with his flesh, blood, nerves, head, and heart, a historically and socially concrete person.

Now it was he who spoke:
"The gates of Seljuk are narrow.
                    You can't come and go.
It has a fortress
                not so easy to raze.
Go away, roan-horsed brave,
                go on your way . . ."

I said: "I can come and go!"
I said: "I can raze and set fires!"
He said: "The rain has ended,
            it's getting light.
    The headsman Ali
        is calling
            Mustafa!
Go away, roan-horsed brave,
                go on your way . . . "

I said: "Friends
        let me go
        let me go.
    Friends
        let me see him
        let me see him!
    Don't think
    I can't take it.
    Don't think
    I can't burn
    without letting it show!

    Friends
    don't say no,
    don't say no uselessly.
    This is not a pear that will snap its stem,

this is no pear;
it won't fall from its branch even if it's wounded,
this heart
this heart is not a sparrow,
        a sparrow!

Friends
I know!
Friends
I know where he is, how he is!
I know
he's gone and won't come back!
I know
he's nailed
by his hands
naked on a bleeding cross
        on the hump of a camel.
Friends
        let me go.
Friends
just let me go and see
see
Bedreddin's man
Börklüje Mustafa
Mustafa."

Two thousand men to be beheaded,
Mustafa and his cross,
headsman, block, and sword —
everything is ready
        everything is set.

                *

A gilt-embroidered red saddlecloth,
gold stirrups,

a gray horse.
On the horse is a thick-browed child,
the ruler of Amasya, Crown Prince Murad.
And next to him,
Bayezid Pasha — I do it on his I-don't-know-whateth decoration!

The headsman struck.
Bare necks split like pomegranates.
Like apples dropping from a green branch,
        heads fell one after another.
And as each head fell,
Mustafa took a last look
from his cross.
And each head that fell
did not turn a hair:
it just said,
        "Come,
                Grand Sultan Mustafa!"
and not a word more . . .

11.

Bayezid Pasha had gone to Manisa and found there Bedreddin's disciple Torlak Kemal, and there he hanged him. The ten provinces were inspected and returned again as fiefs to the sovereign's servant lords.

My guide and I passed through these ten provinces. Vultures circled overhead and, from time to time, with wild shrieks they swooped down in dark streams, descending on the fresh, bloody corpses of women and children. Although the bodies of men young and old lined the roads in the sun, the fact that the birds preferred the flesh of women and children showed how glutted they were.

On the roads, we met the parading troops of the sovereign lords.

As the sovereign's servant lords passed with their loud-colored banners and drums and fanfare through the sluggish winds weighing like the air of a rotting vineyard and returned over the chopped-up earth to settle down on their fiefs, we left the ten provinces. Gallipoli appeared in the distance, and I said to my guide: "I have no strength left. I can't swim across."

We found a boat.

The sea was rough. I looked at the boatman. He looks like the picture I tore out of a German book and hung up on my wall. His thick mustache is ebony-black, and his beard is broad and white. In all my life I've never seen such an open, such an eloquent forehead.

We were in the middle of the strait, the sea flowed on nonstop, the water foamed and slipped under our boat in the lead-painted air, when our boatman who looked like the picture in the cell said:

"Freeman and slave, patrician and plebian, lord and serf, guildmaster and journeyman, in a word, the oppressor and the oppressed, stood in constant opposition to one another and carried on, now covertly, now openly, a constant struggle."

12.
Upon setting foot in Rumelia, we learned that Sultan Mehmet had lifted the siege of Salonika and come to Serrai. We traveled day and night to get to the Mad Forest as soon as possible.

One night when we were resting on the roadside, three horsemen heading away from the Mad Forest rode by at full gallop toward Serrai. In one of the horsemen's saddles I saw a dark shape tied up in a bag, which looked like a person. My hairs rose. I said to my guide:

I know these hoofbeats.
These jet-black horses foaming blood
have carried prisoners tied to their saddles
at full gallop down the dark road.

I know these hoofbeats.
One morning
            they
come up to our tents like a song of friendship.
We break bread with them.
The air is so beautiful,
the heart so hopeful,
the eye is a child again,
and our wise friend, SUSPICION, is asleep . . .

I know these hoofbeats.
One night
         they
ride away from our tents at full speed.
They knife the sentry in the back,
and in one of their saddles,
            arms tied behind his back,
                        is our most precious.

I know these hoofbeats,
and the Mad Forest knows them too . . .

Before long we learned that the Mad Forest did in
fact know these hoofbeats. As soon as we stepped into
our forest we heard that Bayezid Pasha had, with all
the necessary precautions, planted men in the forest
who penetrated the camp, joined Bedreddin's fol-
lowers, and one night, coming upon Bedreddin asleep
in his tent, carried him off. So the three horsemen we
met on the road were the forefathers of all the under-

cover agents in Ottoman history, and the prisoner
they carried in their saddle was Bedreddin.

13.
Rumelia, Serrai,
and an old expression:
    HIS IMPERIAL PRESENCE.

At the center,
straight as a sword stuck in the ground,
                                the old man.
Facing him, the Sultan.
They looked at each other.

It was the Sultan's wish
that, before finishing off this incarnation of blasphemy,
before giving the word to the hangman,
the law should exercise its skills
and the matter be disposed of properly.

A member of the court,
Mevlana Haydar by name,
newly arrived from Persia
                and a man of great learning,
bowed his hennaed beard to divine inspiration
and, saying "This man's substance is unholy,
                        but his blood is holy,"
                    wrapped the matter up.

They turned to Bedreddin.
They said: "You talk now."
They said: "Account for your heresy."

Bedreddin
looked out through the archway.

There's sun outside.
The branches of a tree turning green in the yard,
and a brook carving stones.
Bedreddin smiled.
His eyes lit up,
            he said:
"Since we have lost this time,
words avail not.
Don't draw it out.
Since the sentence is mine,
give it — that I may seal it . . . "

14.
The rain hisses,
scared,
whispering,
like words of betrayal.

The rain hisses,
like the bare white feet of renegades
running on wet dark earth.

The rain hisses.
In the market place of Serrai,
across from the coppersmith's,
Bedreddin hangs from a tree.

The rain hisses.
It's a late and starless hour of the night.
And swinging from a leafless branch,
getting wet in the rain,
            is the naked body of my sheik.

The rain hisses.
The market place is mute,

Serrai is blind.

In the air, the doomed sorrow of not seeing and not speaking.

And the market place of Serrai has covered its face with its hands.

The rain hisses.

The Lathe-Turner Shefik's Shirt

The rain hissed outside. On the horizon of sea beyond the iron bars and in the cloudy sky above, it was morning. I remember it very clearly even today. First I felt a hand on my shoulder. I turned around. The lathe-turner Shefik has fixed his shining, coal-black eyes on my face: "It looks like you didn't sleep last night," he says.

Upstairs, the bandits' chains were quiet. They must have gone to sleep when it got light. In daylight the guards' whistles also lose their meaning. Their colors fade, and their sharp outlines, which show only in the darkness, soften.

The ward door opened from the outside. Inside, the men are waking up one by one.

Shefik asks: "You look a little strange — what happened?"

I tell Shefik my night's adventure: "But," I say, "I saw it with my own eyes. He came right up to this window here. He wore a seamless white robe. He took my hand. I made the whole journey at his side — I mean with his guidance."

Shefik is laughing. He points to the window: "You made your journey not with Mustafa's disciple but with my shirt. Look — I hung it out last night. It's still at the window."

By now I'm laughing too. I take down from the bars Shefik's shirt, which served as my guide in Sheik Bedreddin's movement. Shefik puts his shirt on. Everyone in the ward has heard about my "journey." Ahmet says: "Now this is something you should write down. We want a 'Bedreddin epic.' And I'll tell you a story myself — you can put it at the end of your book."

And here at the end of my book is the story Ahmet told.

Ahmet's Story

It was before the Balkan War. I was nine years old. My grandfather and I were the guests of a peasant in Rumelia. The peasant had blue eyes and a copper beard. We had *tarhana* soup with lots of red pepper. It was winter — one of Rumelia's dry winters that cut like a well-sharpened knife.

I can't remember the name of the village. Except the gendarme who saw us down to the road had described the people of this village as the most stubborn, hardest-to-get-taxes-from, most pigheaded peasants in the world.

According to the gendarme, they're neither Moslems nor infidels. Perhaps they were Kizilbash. But not quite that either.

I still remember going into the village. The sun was just about set, the road frozen. There were red lights on the hard frozen puddles that glittered like glass on the road.

A dog met us at the first barbed-wire fence sinking into the darkness. A huge dog looming even larger in the half-dark. He was barking.

Our driver tightened the reins. The dog attacked the horses, jumping way up to their chests.

"What's happening?" I said, and stuck my head out to see. The driver's elbow hit me in the face as he raised his whip and it cracked down on the dog's head with a snake-hiss. Just then I heard a thick voice.

"Hey! You think you're the governor and anything you hit is a peasant?"

My grandfather got down from the carriage. He said hello to the dog's thick-voiced owner. They talked. Then the blue-eyed, copper-bearded owner of the dog invited us to his house.

I can still hear many conversations from my childhood. I've come to understand what most of them meant only as I've grown older, and I've been surprised at some and laughed or gotten angry at others. But no grownups' talk that I listened to as a child has affected the rest of my life like the talk between my grandfather and the blue-eyed peasant that night.

My grandfather had a soft, gentlemanly voice. The other spoke with a thick, cross, sure voice.

His thick voice said: "Hanging from a leafless branch of a tree in the market place of Serrai by the will of the Sultan and the pronouncement of Judge Haydar from Persia, Bedreddin's naked body slowly swung from side to side. It was night. Three men came around the corner. One led an extra gray horse. Without a saddle. They stopped under the tree Bedreddin hung from. The one on the left took off his shoes. He climbed the tree. The others opened their arms and waited below. The man in the tree started to cut the knot in the wet, soaped rope that wound like a snake around Bedreddin's thin neck under his long white beard. Suddenly the knife slipped off the rope and pierced the stretched neck of the corpse. No blood came. The young man cutting the rope turned white. Then he leaned over and kissed the wound. Throwing the knife away, he undid the knot with his hands, and, like a father leaving his sleeping child in the arms of its mother, he entrusted Bedreddin's body to the arms of those waiting below.

They put the naked body on the bare horse. The man in the tree climbed down. He was the youngest. Leading the bare horse that carried the naked body, he came to our village. He buried the body on the hill, under the black tree. But later the sovereign's horsemen invaded the village. When they left, the young man dug the body up from under the black tree. Thinking they might come back and find the body. And he did not return again."

My grandfather asks: "Are you sure it happened like that?"

"Sure. My mother's father told it to me, and his grandfather had told him. And he heard it from *his* grandfather. It's always been this way . . . . "

There are eight or ten peasants in the room besides us. They sit at the edge of the circle of half-light the fire paints red. Now and then one or another moves, and a hand, part of a face, or a shoulder comes inside the circle of half-light and reddens.

I hear the voice of the copper-beard. "He will come back. The one hung from a tree naked will come back naked."

My grandfather laughs: "This belief of yours," he says, "is like the Christians' faith. They say the prophet Jesus will come back to earth. Even among Moslems there are those who believe Jesus will one day appear in Damascus."

He doesn't answer my grandfather right away. Pushing against his knees with his thick-fingered hands, he straightens up. Now his whole body is inside the red circle. I see his face in profile. He has a long, straight nose. He talks as if fighting: "Jesus is to be reborn with his flesh, bones, beard. This is a lie. Bedreddin will be reborn without his bones, beard, mustache — like the look of an eye, the words of a tongue, the breath of a chest. This I know. We are Bedreddin's men; we don't believe in any afterlife or Resurrection that we should believe a dead, scattered body would gather together and be reborn. When we say Bedreddin will come again, we mean that his words, look, and breath will appear from among us."

He stopped and sat down. Whether my grandfather believed in Bedreddin's return or not, I don't know. I believed it at nine and, at thirty-some years, I still believe it.

LETTERS FROM CHANKIRI PRISON

1
Four o'clock,
              no you.
Five o'clock,
              nothing.
Six, seven,
tomorrow,
the day after,
and maybe —
         who knows. . .

We had a garden
              in the prison yard.
At the foot of a sunny wall,
              about fifteen paces long.
You used to come,
we'd sit side by side,
your big red
         oilcloth bag
                   on your knees. . .
Remember "Head" Mehmet?
From the juveniles ward.
Square head,
thick, short legs,
and hands bigger than his feet.
With a rock he bashed in the head
         of the man whose hive he stole honey from.
He used to call you "Good lady."
He had a garden smaller than ours
                   up there right above us
                             close to the sun,
                   in a tin can.

Do you remember a Saturday,

a late afternoon sprinkled
                    by the prison fountain?
The tinsmith Shaban sang a song,
remember:
    "Beypazari is our home, our city,
    who knows where we'll leave our body. . .?"
I did so many pictures of you,
you didn't leave me even one.
All I have is a photograph:
in another garden,
                very at ease,
                very happy,
    you're feeding some chickens
    and laughing.

There weren't any chickens in the prison garden,
but we could laugh all right
                    and we weren't unhappy.
How we heard news
            of most beautiful freedom,
how we listened for the footsteps
            of good news coming,
what beautiful things we talked
            in the prison garden. . .

2
One afternoon
we sat
by the prison gates
and read Ghazali's rubaiyat:
"The great azure Garden
                of the Night.
The gold-sparkling whirling of the Dancers.
And in wooden boxes the Dead stretched out."

If one day,
far from me,
you find life weighs on you
like a dark rain,
        read Ghazali again.
And, my Pirayé,
I know
you'll have only pity
for his desperate loneliness
        and magnificent fear
        facing death.

Let flowing water bring Ghazali to you:
"— On the Potter's shelf,
        the sovereign is but an earthen Bowl,
        and victories are written
        on the Ruined walls of the king of kings. . . "
Welling up and springing forth.
Cold
      hot
          cool.
And in the great azure garden,
                the endless,
                ceaseless
                whirling of the dancers. . .

I don't know why
there's this saying in my head,
a Chankiri saying
I first heard from you:
"When the poplars fuzz,
                cherries aren't far behind."
The poplars are fuzzing in Ghazali,
but
the master doesn't see

                    the cherries coming.
That's why he worships death.

Upstairs, "Sugar" Ali plays his music.
Evening.
Outside, everybody's shouting.
Water is flowing from the fountain.
And in the light of the guardhouse,
tied to the acacias, three baby wolves.
Beyond the bars,
            my great, azure garden opened up.
W h a t   i s   r e a l   i s   l i f e . . .

Don't forget me, Pirayé. . .

3
Wednesday today —
you know,
Chankiri's market day.
It will even reach us,
passing through our iron door in reed baskets:
its eggs, bulgur,
its gilded purple eggplants. . .

Yesterday
I watched them coming down from the villages:
tired,
wily,
            and suspicious,
with sorrow under their brows.
They passed by — the men on donkeys,
the women on their bare feet.
You probably know some of them.

And the last two Wednesdays they've probably looked
          around the market for the red-scarfed,
          "not-uppity" lady from Istanbul. . .

7.20.1940

4
The heat is like nothing you've ever known,
and I who grew up by the sea —
the sea is so far away. . .

Between two and five
I lie under the mosquito netting
soaking wet
motionless
eyes open
and listen to the flies buzzing.
I know
in the yard now
they're throwing water on the walls,
the hot, red stones are steaming.
And outside, skirting the burnt grass
of the fortress, the black-
bricked city sits
in nitric acid light. . .

Nights a wind comes up suddenly
and then suddenly dies.
And panting like a living thing in the darkness,
the heat moves around on soft, furry feet,
threatening us with something.
And from time to time
we shiver feeling on our skin
                    nature afraid. . .

There might be an earthquake.
It's already within three days of us.
The danger rocked Yozgat.
And the people here say:
because it's built on a salt mine,
          the city of Chankiri will collapse
                    forty days before doomsday.
To go to bed one night
and not wake up in the morning,
                    your head smashed by a wooden beam.
What a blind, good-for-nothing death.
I want to live a little longer —
a good deal longer.
I want this for many things,
for many
very important things.

                                        8.12.1940

5
It gets dark at five
with clouds on the attack.
It's clear they carry rain.
Many
pass low enough to touch.
The hundred watts in our room
and the tailors' oil lamp are on.
The tailors are drinking linden tea. . .
It means winter's here. . .
I'm cold.
But not sad.
This is a privilege reserved for us:
on winter days in prison,
and not just in prison

but in this vast world
    which should —
        which will —
           be warm,
                to be cold
                but not sad. . .

10.26.1940

LETTER TO KEMAL TAHIR

I say "Malatya,"
    and all I can think of are your beetle-brows.
  Hot springs of Bursa,
        apples of Amasya,
           scorpions and watermelons of Diyarbakir,
but what's where you are,
        Malatya,
        famous for —
which of its fruits and bugs,
      its water or its air?
Imagine, I don't even know anything about its prison.
Only this:
one room,
with just one window
        close to the very high ceiling.
You are there
like a little fish
        in a tall, narrow jar. . .
You may not like my simile.
Especially these days
        you probably think you're a lion in a cage.
You're right, Kemal Tahir,
you can be sure I do too,
sure we're lions
— I'm not kidding —
        and what's even more terrific,
           we're human. . .
And we both know
      at what time and from which class. . .
Still, this doesn't change the business about the iron cage
          and the jar —
          they're both the same,
          especially these days. . .

— Only the one lying inside comfortable and safe
                                    knows this — . . .
Especially these days,
to laugh at the jokes of Emin Bey from Sariyer,
the taste of loved books and tomatoes,
sleep in spite of bedbugs
        — even if it's with three teaspoons of Adonille a day —
and, Tahir's son Kemal,
even a letter from you
and even to hear sounds, to touch, to be able to see the light
                                    of the air —
any comforts to myself,
            beyond my love for my wife,
                        I can't forgive. . .
Hypersensitive?
No.
Not to be able to fight,
not even as much as a Mauser bullet,
                            in fact
                                    and directly. . .
Only the one hit in battle feels no pain,
and the freedom to fight
                        is the most important freedom.
I'm burning inside, Kemal,
                and cool on the outside. . .
You understand —
anyway all this talk
                is just more of our talk:
it's been said lots of times
                        and is still being said. . .
Who knows how many people in how many places
— cursing and pitying their hands lying idle and helpless
                                on their knees —
                        are talking like this now. . .
You understand,

but no matter —
I'm going to say it anyway!
The base consolation of talking and explaining
                    when one can do nothing?
Maybe yes,
maybe no. . .
No, it's not like that.
What consolation, for God's sake come off it. . .
This is strictly
pacing in circles, head down,
and roaring and bellowing and shouting, Kemal. . .

1941, Fall

9-10 P.M. POEMS

How beautiful to remember you:
amid news of death and victory,
in prison,
and when I'm past forty. . .

How beautiful to remember you:
your hand forgotten on a blue cloth
and in your hair
the grave softness of my beloved earth of Istanbul. . .
The happiness of loving you
    is like a second person inside me. . .
The fragrance of the geranium leaf that stays on the fingertips,
a sunny quiet,
and the call of flesh:
    a warm,
        deep darkness
            parted by bright red lines. . .

How beautiful to remember you,
to write about you,
to lie back in prison and think of you:
what you said on this or that day in such and such a place,
        not the words themselves
            but the world in their aura. . .

How beautiful to remember you.
I must carve you something from wood again —
        a box,
           a ring —
and I must weave about three meters of fine silk.
And jumping
    right up
and grabbing hold of the iron bars at my window,

I must shout out the things I write for you
　　　　　　to the milk-white blue of freedom. . .

How beautiful to remember you:
amid news of death and victory,
in prison,
and when I'm past forty. . .

20 September 1945

At this late hour
this fall night
　　　　　　I am full of your words:
words
　　　　eternal like time and matter,
　　　　　　　naked like eyes,
　　　　　　　　　heavy like hands,
　　　and sparkling like stars.

Your words came to me,
they were from your heart, mind, and flesh.
Your words brought you,
　　　　　　they were: mother,
　　　　　　　　　woman,
　　　　　　　　　　　and comrade.
They were sad, painful, happy, they were hopeful, brave —
　　　　　　　　your words were *human*. . .

21 September 1945

Our son is sick,
his father's in prison,
your head is heavy in your tired hands —
our state is like the world's. . .

People carry people to better days,
our son gets well,
his father gets out of prison,
the insides of your gold eyes laugh —
our state is like the world's. . .

22 September 1945

I read a book:
         you are in it;
I listen to a song:
         you're in it.
I sit eating my bread:
         you sit facing me;
I work:
         you're facing me.
You who are everywhere my "Ever Present,"
         I cannot talk with you,
         we cannot hear each other's voice:
you are my eight-year widow. . .

23 September 1945

What is she doing now,
         right now, this instant?
Is she in the house or outside?
Is she working, lying down, standing up?
Maybe she's just raised her arm
— hey, my rose,
         how this suddenly bares her thick white wrist!

What is she doing now,
         right now, this instant?

Maybe there's a kitten on her lap,
                        she's petting it.
Or maybe she's walking, about to take a step
— the beloved feet that take her straight to me
                        on each of my dark days!
And what is she thinking of —
                        me?
Or —
        I don't know —
                why the beans refuse to cook?
Or else
        why most people are unhappy like this?

What is she thinking now,
                right now, this instant?

24 September 1945

The most beautiful sea
                        hasn't been crossed yet.
The most beautiful child
                        hasn't grown up yet.
Our most beautiful days
                we haven't lived yet.
And the most beautiful words I wanted to tell you
                I haven't said yet. . .

25 September 1945

9 o'clock.
The bell struck in the town square,
the ward doors will close any minute.
Prison has been a little long this time:
                        8 years. . .

74

To live — it's a hopeful thing, my love.
To live —
            it's a serious thing, like loving you. . .

26 September 1945

They've taken us prisoner,
they've thrown us in jail:
            me inside the walls,
                  you outside.
But this is nothing.
The worst thing
is for a person — knowingly or not —
to carry prison inside himself. . .
Most people have been forced into this position,
honest, hard-working, good people,
who deserve to be loved as much as I love you. . .

30 September 1945

To think of you is a beautiful thing,
                        a hopeful thing,
something like listening to the most beautiful song
                        from the best voice in the world.
But hope is no longer enough for me,
I no longer want to listen —
            I want to sing the songs. . .

1 October 1945

Over the mountain:
there's a cloud flush with evening sun over the mountain.

Today too:
today too passed without you, I mean without half the world.
Soon they'll open
red on red:
soon the four-o'clocks will open red on red.
In the air brave, silent wings carry
        our separation, which feels like exile. . .

2 October 1945

The wind flows on,
the same cherry branch doesn't bend in the same wind even once.
Birds chirp in the tree:
                the wings want to fly.
The door is closed:
                it wants to break open.
I want you:
that life be
beautiful like you,
        friendly and loving. . .
I know the feast of poverty
                still is not over. . .
It will be yet. . .

5 October 1945

We both know, my love,
they taught us:
        how to be hungry, cold,
        tired to death,
        and apart from each other.
We haven't been forced to kill yet,
and we haven't been through the business of being killed.

76

We both know, my love,
we can teach:
>> how to fight for our people
>> and how — each day
>>>> a little deeper, a little better —
>>>>>> *to love. . .*

6 October 1945

Clouds pass loaded with news, heavy.
The letter that hasn't come crumples in my hand.
The heart is at the tips of the eyelashes,
>> blessing the earth that lengthens and disappears.
I want to call out: "P i r a y é ,
>>>> P i r a y é ! . . . "

7 October 1945

Human cries crossed the open seas at night
>>>> with
>>>>>> the winds.
It's still not safe
>> to travel the open seas at night. . .

Six years this field hasn't been plowed,
the tracks of the tank treads stay in the earth.
The tracks of the tank treads
>> will be covered with snow this winter.

Ah, light of my life,
the antennas are lying again —
so the merchants of sweat
>> can close the books with a hundred-percent profit.

But those who came back from the table of the Angel of Death
came back with sealed fates. . .

8 October 1945

I've become impossible again:
            sleepless, irritable, perverse.
Today,
as if cursing all that's holy, as if beating a mad beast,
                        I work all day,
    and the next day
I lie on my back from morning to night,
    a lazy song like an unlit cigarette in my mouth.
And it drives me wild,
            the hatred
                and pity I feel for myself. . .

I've become impossible again:
            sleepless, irritable, perverse.
Again, as always, I'm wrong.
There's no reason,
                and there couldn't be.
What I'm doing is shameful,
                    a disgrace.
But I can't help it:
                I'm jealous of you,
                forgive me. . .

9 October 1945

Last night you were in my dream:
you were sitting at my knee.
You raised your head and turned your huge yellow eyes to me.

You were asking something.
Your moist lips open and close,
                    but I don't hear your voice.

Somewhere in the night a clock strikes like bright news.
In the air, the whisper of no beginning and no end.
I hear: "Memo" 's song — my canary — in his red cage,
the crackling of seeds pushing through the soil in a plowed field,
and the righteous, triumphant hum of a crowd.
Your moist lips still open and close,
                    but I don't hear your voice. . .

I woke up broken.
I had fallen asleep over the book.
I think:
        Could it be all those voices were your voice?

10 October 1945

When I look into your eyes
        the smell of sunny earth hits me:
        I'm in a wheatfield, lost in the grain.

An endless green-glittering abyss,
your eyes are like always-changing eternal matter,
                which gives away its secret a little every day
                but will never
                totally surrender. . .

18 October 1945

As we go forth from the castle door to meet death,
we'll be able to say these words, my love,

to the city we turn to look at for the last time:
"Even if you didn't make us smile all that much,
we did what we could
that you might be
happy.
Your way to happiness goes on,
life goes on.
We're at peace,
in our heart the satisfaction of your earned bread,
in our eyes the sadness of leaving your light,
we came and here we're going,
be of good cheer, city of Aleppo. . ."

27 October 1945

We are one half of an apple,
the other half is this huge world.
We are one half of an apple,
the other half is our people.
You are one half of an apple,
the other half is me,
us two. . .

28 October 1945

The swelling fragrance of the rose geranium,
the humming of the seas,
and here with its full clouds and wise earth is fall. . .

My love,
the years have ripened.
It strikes me we've lived
the adventures maybe of a thousand-year life.

80

But we are still
      wide-eyed children
          running barefoot hand-in-hand in the sun. . .

5 November 1945

Forget the flowering almonds.
It's not worth it:
in this business
      what cannot come back should not be remembered.
Dry your wet hair in the sun:
      let the moist, heavy reds glow
          with the languor of ripe fruit. . .
My love, my love,
      the season
          fall. . .

8 November 1945

Over the rooftops of my faraway city
under the Sea of Marmara
and across the fall earth
          your voice came
             ripe and moist.
For three minutes.
Then the telephone went black. . .

12 November 1945

The last south winds started,
      warm and humming like blood spurting from an artery.

I listen to the air:
             the pulse has slowed.
There's snow on Mount Uludağ,
and on Cherry Hill the bears have gone to sleep
             on red chestnut leaves, cuddly and grand.
On the plain the poplars are undressing.
The silkworm eggs are just about in for the winter,
fall is just about over,
the earth is about to enter its pregnant sleep.
And we will pass another winter:
             in our great anger
             and warmed by the fire of our sacred hope. . .

13 November 1945

The poverty of Istanbul — they say — defies description,
hunger — they say — ravaged the people,
TB — they say — is everywhere.
Little girls this high — they say —
             in burned-out buildings, movie theaters. . .

Dark news comes from my faraway city,
the city of honest, hard-working, poor people —
                           my real Istanbul,
which is your home, my love,
and which I take with me in the bag on my back
      wherever I'm exiled, to whatever prison I'm lying in,
      the city I carry in my heart like the loss of a child,
      like your image in my eyes. . .

20 November 1945

Though there's still an occasional carnation in the flowerpots,

the fall plowing is long over on the plain:
                        they're sowing seeds now.
And picking olives.
Both moving into winter
and making room for the spring shoots.
And me, full of you
            and loaded with the impatience of great journeys,
            I'm lying in Bursa like an anchored freighter. . .

The Fourth of December of 1945

Take out the dress I first saw you in,
look your best,
look like spring trees. . .
Wear in your hair
        the carnation I sent you in a letter from prison,
raise your kissable, lined, wide white forehead.
On a day like this, not broken and sad —
                        no way! —
on a day like this, Nazim Hikmet's woman must be beautiful
                    like a flag of rebellion . . .

5 December 1945

The bilge has busted,
the slaves break their chains.
That's a northeaster blowing,
it'll smash the hull on the rocks.
This world, this pirate ship, will sink —
            come hell or high water, it will sink.
And we will build a world as hopeful, free,
            and open as your forehead, my Pirayé. . .

6 December 1945

They are the enemies of hope, my love,
enemies of flowing water,
    of the fertile tree,
    of life growing and unfolding.
Death has marked them:
        the rotting tooth, the falling flesh —
    they will be gone, never to return.
And yes, my love,
it will walk around swinging its arms
in its most glorious clothes, the overalls of workers —
        yes, freedom in this beautiful country...

7 December 1945

Enemy of Rejeb, the towel man in Bursa,
of the fitter Hasan in the Karabük factory,
enemy of the poor peasant woman Hatije,
of the day laborer Süleyman,
your enemy, my enemy,
the enemy of anyone who thinks,
and this country, the home of these people —
my love, they are the enemy of this country...

12 December 1945

The trees on the plain are making one last effort to shine:
        spangled gold
         copper
          bronze and wood...
The feet of the oxen sink softly into the moist earth.

And the mountains are dipped in smoke:
                  lead-gray, soaking wet. . .
That's it,
fall must be finally over today.
Wild geese just shot by,
                they're probably headed for Iznik Lake.
In the air, a coolness,
      in the air something like the smell of soot:
      the smell of snow is in the air.

To be outside now,
      to ride a horse at full gallop toward the mountains. . .
You'll say, "You don't know how to ride a horse,"
but don't joke
         and don't be jealous:
I've acquired a new habit in prison,
I love nature — if not as much,
              nearly as much — as I love you.
              And both of you are far away. . .

13 December 1945

At night snow came on suddenly.
Morning was crows exploding from snow-white branches.
As far as the eye can see, winter on the Bursa plain:
one thinks of what has no beginning and no end.
My love,
the season's changed
         in one leap after great labor.
And under the snow, proud,
             hard-working
                 life goes on. . .

14 December 1945

Damn it, winter has come on hard. . .
You and my honest Istanbul, who knows how you are?
Do you have coal?
Could you buy wood?
Line the windows with newspaper.
Go to bed early.
There must be nothing left in the house to sell.
To be cold and still half hungry:
        in this too we are the majority
        in the world, our country, and our city. . .

NINTH ANNIVERSARY

One night of knee-deep snow
my adventure started —
pulled from the suppertable,
put into a police car,
sent off on a train,
and locked up in a room.
Its ninth year was over three days ago.

In the corridor, a man on a stretcher
is dying open-mouthed on his back,
the grief of long iron years in his face.

One thinks of isolation
                — sickening and total,
                        like that of the mad and the dead —
first, seventy-six days
        in the silent hostility of the door that closed on me,
and then seven weeks in the steerage of a ship.
Still, we weren't defeated:
my head
        was a second person at my side.

I've completely forgotten most of their faces
— all I remember is a very long, very thin nose —
yet how many times they lined up before me.
When my sentence was read they had one worry:
                                to look imposing.
                                They did not.
They looked more like things than people:
like wall clocks, stupid
                and arrogant,
and sad and pitiful like handcuffs, chains, etc.

A city without houses or streets.
Tons of hope, tons of grief.

The distances microscopic.
Of the four-legged creatures, just cats.

I'm in a world of forbidden things!
To smell the lover's cheek:
                    forbidden.
To eat at the same table with your children:
                    forbidden.
To talk with your brother or your mother
     without a wire screen and a guard standing between you:
                    forbidden.
To seal the envelope of the letter you've written,
or to get a letter still sealed:
                    forbidden.
To turn off the light when you go to bed:
                    forbidden.
To play backgammon:
                    forbidden.
And not that it isn't forbidden,
     but what you can hide in your heart and have in your hand
          is to love, to think, and to understand.

In the corridor, the man on the stretcher died.
They took him away.
Now no hope, no grief,
               no bread, no water,
               no freedom, no prison,
               no wanting women, no guards, no bedbugs,
               and no more cats to sit and stare at him.
                    This business is finished, over.

But ours goes on:
my head goes on loving, thinking, understanding,
the pitiless rage of not being able to fight keeps up,
and since morning the ache in my liver goes on. . .

                                        1946

HAZEL ARE MY LADY'S EYES

Hazel are my lady's eyes,
the wavy greens of watered silk inside:
on gold leaf, green-on-green *moiré*.
Brothers, what's going on here,
these nine years our hands haven't touched,
I got old here,
she there.

My girl whose thick, white neck is wrinkling,
it's impossible for us to get old,
we need another term for the slackening of flesh,
because to get old
means to love no one but yourself.

1947

I LOVE YOU

I kneeled down, I'm looking at the earth,
I'm looking at the grass,
I'm looking at insects,
I'm looking at tiny branches blooming with blues.
You are like the spring earth, my love,
                    I'm looking at you.

I lie on my back, I see the sky,
I see the branches of the tree,
I see the flying storks,
I see a dream with my eyes open.
You are like the sky in spring,
                    I see you.

At night I light a fire in the field, I touch fire,
I touch water,
I touch cloth,
I touch silver.
You are like the fire lit under the stars,
                    I touch you.

I am among people, I love people,
I love motion,
I love thought,
I love my struggle.
You are a person in my struggle,
                    I love you.

1947

ON IBRAHIM BALABAN'S "SPRING PICTURE"

Here, eyes, see Balaban's skill.
Here is dawn. We're in the month of May.
Here is light:
        smart, brave, fresh, alive, pitiless.
Here are clouds:
        like whipped cream.
Here, mountains: blue even, and cool.
Here are foxes on their morning rounds,
light on their long tails,
        alarm on their pointed noses.
Here, eyes, see:
hungry, hairs raised, red-mouthed,
here on a mountaintop, a wolf.
Haven't you ever felt in yourself
the rage of a hungry wolf at morning?
Here, eyes, see: butterflies, bees,
the whirl of sparkling fish.
Here, a stork
        just back from Egypt.
Here is a deer,
        creature of a more beautiful world.
Here, eyes, see the bear in front of its den,
        still sleepy.
Hasn't it ever occurred to you, ever?
To live unconsciously like bears, smelling the earth,
close to pears and the mossy dimness,
far from human voices and fire?
Here, eyes, see: squirrels, rabbits,
lizards, turtles,
our grape-eyed donkey.
Here, eyes, see
a shimmering tree,
in its beauty most like a person.

Here is green grass:
                    go on in, my bare feet.
Here, nose, smell:
                    mint, thyme.
Here, mouth, water:
                    sorrels, mallows.
Touch, hands, caress, hold,
here, my mother's milk,
          my wife's flesh,
                    my child's smile.
Here is plowed earth,
here is man:
lord of rocks and mountains, the birds and the beasts.
Here are his sandals, here the patches on his breeches.
Here is the plow,
here are the oxen, on their rumps the sad, terrible sores.

1947

HYMN TO LIFE

The hair falling on your forehead
suddenly scattered.
Suddenly something moved on the ground:
the trees are talking something
in the dark.
Your bare arms will be cold.
Far away,
where we can't see,
the moon must be rising.
It hasn't reached us yet,
falling through the leaves
and lighting up your shoulder.
But I know wind
comes up with the moon.
The trees are talking.
Your bare arms will be cold.

From above,
from the branches lost in the dark,
something fell at your feet.
You moved closer to me.
Under my hand your bare flesh is like the fuzzy skin of a fruit.
Neither a song of the heart nor "common sense" —
before the trees, birds, and insects,
on my wife's flesh
my hand is thinking.
Tonight my hand
can't read or write.
Neither unloving nor loving. . .
It's the tongue of a leopard at a spring,
it's a grape leaf,
a wolf's paw.
To move, to breathe, to eat, to drink.

My hand is like a seed
splitting open underground.
Neither a song of the heart nor common sense,
neither unloving nor loving.
Thinking on my wife's flesh
is the hand of the first man.
Like a root that finds water underground,
it says to me:
"To eat, to drink, cold, hot, struggle, smell, color,
not to live in order to die,
but to die to live. . ."

And now
as red female hair blows across my face,
as something moves on the ground,
as the trees talk something in the dark,
and as the moon rises far away
where we can't see,
my hand on my wife's flesh,
before the trees, birds, and insects,
I want the right of what is called life,
of the leopard at the spring, of the seed splitting open,
I want the right of the first man.

1947

I MADE A JOURNEY

At night, far off in the distance,
        the lights of the airports burned into the sky
like a white fire,
and the trains I missed — taking things from me —
        dived sparkling into the darkness.
I made a journey.

I made a journey.
The eyes of the people were all white,
the putrid waters stank.
I passed through the swamp of lies and stupidity
        without getting lost in the head-high reeds. . .

I made a journey —
with the women sitting doubled over,
        their fists on their flat bellies,
or running barefoot ahead of the wind;
with the dead;
with those forgotten on battlefields and barricades.

I made a journey,
riding on trucks
        taking prisoners
            through cities,
                the asphalt moist with the morning light. . .

I made a journey,
I could not get enough of the grapes crushed by your white teeth
or of your bed like a shuttered summer afternoon.

I made a journey —
there were brand-new buildings in the warehouses,
hope was bright green like a young pine,

and lamps burned on foreheads
    a thousand meters underground.

I made a journey,
in moonlight, in sunlight,
in the light of the rain,
with the four seasons and all time,
with the insects, grasses, and stars,
and with the most honest people of the earth —
I mean, affectionate like a violin,
pitiless like a child who can't yet speak,
brave like a child who can't yet speak,
I mean, ready with the ease of a bird to die
    or live a thousand years. . .

1948

OCCUPATION

As the dawn breaks on the horns of my ox,
I plow the earth with patient pride.
The earth is moist and warm on my bare feet.

I beat iron all morning —
the darkness is dyed red.

In the afternoon heat I pick olives,
the leaves the loveliest of greens:
I'm light from head to toe.

Guests come without fail each evening,
my door is wide open
                    to all songs.

At night I wade knee-deep into the water
and pull the nets out of the sea:
the fish get all mixed up with the stars.

Now I am accountable
                    for the state of the world:
people and earth, darkness and light.

So you see I'm up to my ears in work.
Don't bother me with talk, my rose,
I'm busy falling in love with you.

1948

POEM

I'm inside the advancing light,
my hands are hungry, the world beautiful.

My eyes can't get enough of the trees —
they're so hopeful, so green.

A sunny road runs through the mulberries,
I'm at the window of the prison infirmary.

I can't smell the medicines —
carnations must be blooming somewhere.

It's like this:
being captured is beside the point,
the point is not to surrender.

1948

POEM

Is this sadness I feel
    these sunny winter days
    the longing to be places I'm not —
on the bridge in my Istanbul, for instance,
or among the workers in Adana,
or in the Greek mountains, or in China,
or next to the one who no longer loves me?

Or is it a trick
        of my liver,
or has a dream thrown me into this state,
or is it that loneliness has come down on me again,
or that I'm pushing fifty,
                is that it?

The second chapter
of this sadness I feel
    will tiptoe out
           and go the way it came —
just so I finish this writing
or sleep a little better,
just so a letter comes,
or some news on the radio. . .

1949

ABOUT YOUR HANDS AND LIES

Your hands grave like all stones,
sad like all songs sung in prison,
clumsy and heavy like all beasts of burden,
your hands that are like the sullen faces of hungry children.
Your hands nimble and light like bees,
full like breasts with milk,
brave like nature,
your hands that hide their friendly softness under their rough
skin.
This world doesn't rest on the horns of a bull,
this world rests on your hands.
People, oh my people,
they feed you with lies.
But you're hungry,
you need to be fed with meat and bread.
And never once eating a full meal at a white table,
you leave this world where every branch is loaded with fruit.
Oh my people,
especially those in Asia, Africa,
the Near East, Middle East, Pacific islands
and my countrymen —
I mean, more than seventy percent of all people —
you are old and absent-minded like your hands,
you are curious, amazed, and young like your hands.
Oh my people,
my European, my American,
you are awake, bold, and forgetful like your hands,
like your hands you're quick to seduce,
easy to deceive. . .

People, oh my people,
if the antennas are lying,
if the presses are lying,

if the books lie,
if the poster on the wall and the ad in the column lie,
if the naked thighs of girls on the white screen lie,
if the prayer lies,
if the lullaby lies,
if the dream is lying,
if the violin player at the tavern is lying,
if the moonlight on the nights of hopeless days lies,
if the voice lies,
if the word lies,
if everything but your hands,
        if everyone, is lying,
it's so your hands will be obedient like clay,
blind like darkness,
stupid like sheep dogs,
        it's so your hands won't rebel.
And it's so that in this mortal, this livable world
        — where we are guests so briefly anyway —
        this merchant's empire, this cruelty, won't end.

1949

A SORRY FREEDOM

You sell the care of your eyes and the light of your hands,
you knead the bread of all happiness
    without tasting so much as a crumb,
with your great freedom you work in the houses of strangers,
with the freedom to make a Croesus of him who works you to
                        death you are free.

They stand over you from the day you are born,
they grind out lies nonstop as long as you live,
with your great freedom you think, your finger on your temple,
    with the freedom of conscience
                you are free.

Your head hanging as if cut at the neck,
your arms drooping down on both sides,
with your great freedom you wander around,
with the freedom to be unemployed
                you are free.

Acting as your next friend, they give away your country —
one day, for example, they sign it over to America
along with you and your great freedom,
    with the freedom to be an air base
                you are free.

The damned hands of Wall Street grab you by the collar,
one day you may be sent, say, to Korea,
with your great freedom you might fill a hole,
    with the freedom to be an unknown soldier
                you are free.

You say one shouldn't live like a tool, a number, a means,
but like a human being —

with your great freedom they slap on the cuffs,
     with the freedom to be arrested, imprisoned, and even
          hanged you are free.

You don't have an iron, wood, or tulle curtain in your life,
you don't need to choose freedom —
you are free.
This freedom, it's a sorry thing under the stars.

1951

ABOUT THE SEA

A jumble of jagged mountains fell behind us in the west.
Our train came down into the warm, wet flat plain.
A pickup sweated past us on our right.
The driver was a dark, plump woman in a green dress.
A sailor sat on the burlap sacks in the back,
the ribbon of his cap flailed in the wind.
With its bridges, towers, chimneys, and smoke,
a silvery factory passed on our left
like a warship returning to port.

First came its coolness,
mixing the sharp smell of iodine
with the smell of apples on the racks.
Then I saw it reflected in the sky,
the air got bluer and bluer.
Then suddenly we were face to face.
It was inside the breakwater,
squeezed between the ships and the docks.
I thought of an eagle I saw at the zoo,
his wings drooping at his sides,
his sullen head on his chest.

The train entered the station, it disappeared.
The train left the station, again we were suddenly face to face:
it was dawn.
There the cold, steely gleam
that studied us through slit-eyes
softened and warmed up as it came closer.
I didn't look at it and think:
Our life flares up and dies out like the foam
on this boundless, endless motion.
I wanted to jump out of the car
and run to it, breathless.

Whether in moonlight or in broad daylight,
whether it's like a sheet or foaming and frothing,
to stand on the shore and watch it
kills me.
I feel inside me the sadness of an empty seashell.
I have to be at the center of its eye,
at the nets, say, with the fishermen.
Or else, my hand on the tiller,
                under sail
                        with the lover.
Or else at the captain's side in the storm,
or swimming against the current.
I have to be at the center of its eye.

I thought of Engels.
How beautiful to have our ashes scattered on the ocean.
But me, I want to be put in a pine box
and buried on the Anatolian plateau.
At cherry-time,
sailors from many different ships
can come as guests to our plateau.
And they can sing the same great song
of many different seas.

1954, Moscow Station,
Tbilisi-Moscow trains

MORNING IN PRAGUE

In Prague it's getting light
and snowing —
        sleety,
         leaden.
In Prague the baroque slowly lights up:
                uneasy, distant,
        its gilt grief-blackened.
The statues on the Charles the Fourth bridge
    look like birds descended from a dead star.

In Prague the first trolley has left the garage,
its windows lit up yellow and warm.
But I know
        it's ice-cold inside:
it hasn't been warmed by the breath of the first passenger yet.
In Prague Pepik drinks his coffee and milk,
the wooden table is spotless in the white kitchen.
In Prague it's getting light
and snowing —
        sleety,
         leaden.

In Prague a cart passes —
            a one-horse wagon —
      in front of the Jewish cemetery.
The cart is loaded with longing for another city,
            I am the driver.
In Prague the baroque slowly lights up:
                uneasy, distant,
      its gilt grief-blackened.
In the Jewish cemetery in Prague, death breathless, silent.
Ah my rose, ah my rose,
exile is worse than death. . .

20 .XII .1956

OPTIMISTIC PRAGUE

1957, January 17.
Nine o'clock exactly.
Sun-bright dry cold, no lies,
dry cold rose-pink,
sky-blue dry cold.
My red mustache nearly freezes.
The city of Prague is etched on cut glass
    with a diamond point.
If I touch it, it will ring:
    gold-edged, clear, white.
It's exactly nine o'clock
    on all the towers
        and my watch.
Dry cold sun-bright, rose-pink,
sky-blue dry cold.
It's exactly nine o'clock.
This minute, this second,
    not a single lie was uttered in Prague.
This minute, this second,
    women gave birth without pain,
and not a single hearse
    went down a single street.
This second
    all the charts climbed
    in favor of the sick.
For a moment
    all women were beautiful, all men wise,
    and the manikins not sad.
Now
    children answered all the questions in school
    without stammering.
Now
    there was coal in all the stoves,
    heat in all the radiators,

and the dome of the Black Tower
was covered with gold once again.
For a moment
the blind forgot their darkness,
the hunchbacks their hunches.
For a moment
I didn't have any enemies,
and no one was thinking
the old days might come back.
Now
Wenceslaus came down from his bronze horse,
he mixed with the crowd,
one couldn't tell which was him.
For a moment
you loved me
like you've never loved anyone. . .
This minute, this second,
sun-bright dry cold, no lies,
dry cold rose-pink,
sky-blue dry cold.
The city of Prague is etched on cut glass
with a diamond point.
If I touch it, it will ring:
gold-edged, clear, white.

THE THING CALLED PRAGUE

The thing called Prague is a silver mirror.
I look once,
and it shows me in my twenties.
I am like leaping,
I am like thirty-two healthy teeth,
                    and the world is a walnut.
But there is nothing I want for myself,
all I want is for the girl I love to touch my fingers,
        on her fingers is the greatest secret of the world.
My hands break the bread bigger for my friends,
                    less for myself.
I kiss all the eyes with trachoma
        in the villages of Anatolia.
Somewhere in the world I fall,
        a martyr to the world revolution.
They pass my heart
        on a velvet cushion
            like a Medal of the Red Flag.
The bands play a funeral march.
We bury our dead in the earth
                    under a wall
                    like fertile seeds.
And on top of the earth our songs
            are neither Turkish nor Russian nor English —
                        they're songs.
Lenin lies sick in a snowy forest,
his brows knitted: he thinks of certain people,
he looks into the white darkness,
                    he sees the coming days.
I am like leaping.
I am like thirty-two healthy teeth,
                    and the world is a walnut
                    with a steel shell
                        but full of good news.

The thing called Prague is a silver mirror.
I look again,
and it shows me on my deathbed.
Beads of sweat like drops of wax on my forehead,
my arms stretched out at my sides.
The wallpaper is green.
In the window, the sooty roofs of a big city —
they aren't the roofs of Istanbul.
My eyes are open,
they haven't closed them yet,·
no one knows yet.
Bend down,
look into my pupils:
you'll see a young woman,
she waits alone at a rainy bus stop.
Close my eyes,
            comrade, leave the room
                        on tiptoes.

1957

BOR HOTEL

No way you can sleep nights in Varna,
no way you can sleep:
for the wealth of stars,
for their closeness, their brilliance,
for the rustle of dead waves on the sand,
the rustle of salty weeds
with their pearly shells
and pebbles,
for the sound of the motorboat throbbing like a heart on the sea,
for the memories filling my room,
memories coming from Istanbul,
            passing through the Bosporus,
                    and filling my room,
some with green eyes,
some in handcuffs,
some holding a handkerchief,
the handkerchief smells of lavender.
No way you can sleep in Varna, my love,
in Varna in the Bor Hotel.

2 June 1957

I GOT A LETTER FROM MÜNEVVER SAYING:

Nazim, tell me about the city I was born in.
I left Sofia when I was very small,
but they say I knew Bulgarian. . .
What kind of a city is Sofia?
I used to hear from my mother
Sofia was tiny,
it must have grown —
think,
        it's been forty-one years.
There was a "Park Boris" then.
My nanny used to take me there mornings.
It must be the biggest park in Sofia.
I still have pictures of me taken there.
A park with lots of sun and lots of shade.
Go and sit there.
Maybe you'll run into the bench I played around.
But benches wouldn't last forty years,
they must have rotted and been changed.
Trees are best,
trees live longer than memories.
Go and sit there one day under the oldest chestnut.
Forget about everything,
even our separation,
just think of me.

1957

I WROTE A LETTER TO MÜNEVVER SAYING:

The trees are standing, the old benches are dead.
"Park Boris" has become "Freedom Park."
Under the chestnut I just thought of you,
just you, I mean Memet,
just you and Memet, I mean my country. . .

1957

ELEGY FOR MIKHAIL REFILI

This is the leaf-fall of my generation,
most of us won't make winter.

He went crazy, Refili,
when he got the news. . .
What was I saying. . .
             Do you remember, Mikhail. . .
but you don't have memory now,
you don't have nose, mouth, eyes. . .
Brother, you're a pile of bones
             in a cemetery in Baku.
What was I saying. . .
In Moscow, at our place, one New Year's Eve,
at the table, under the decked-out pine,
you glowed like a huge toy.
Your shining eyes, bald head,
             respectable belly.
Outside, a snowy forest plunged in night.
I looked at you and thought:
    His excellency — pleased as an old barrel of wine,
    hardy as an old wine barrel.
    He's going to live long after me.
    And after me he'll turn out an article
             or a poem:
    "I met Nazim in Moscow in 1924. . ."
Really, Mikhail, you could've been a poet,
             you were a professor.
But that's not the point.
The best of the work we do, or the worst,
             lives after us.
Yours was middling, I think.
Mine too.

I mean, we don't have the consolation that our voices
will remain in this sphere.
For my part, I don't mind.
I've succeeded in living without consolation,
and I'll succeed in dying without consolation —
like you, Refili.

5 June 1958,
Prague

BEES

The bees are big drops of honey,
they carry grapevines to the sun,
they came flying out of my youth,
the apples, these heavy apples,
    are from there too,
this gold-dust road,
these white pebbles in the stream,
my faith in songs,
my being without envy,
the cloudless day, this blue day,
    is from there too,
the sea flat on its back naked and warm,
this longing, these bright teeth and thick lips —
like big drops of honey
on the legs of bees
they came to this Caucasian village
from my youth, the youth I left somewhere
    before I was through.

13 September 1958,
Arhipo Osipovka

EARLY LIGHT

In the early light, telegraph poles,
                              the road.
The dresser with its mirror brightening in the early light,
                              the table,
                              slippers —
things see and know each other once again.
In our room the early light spreads like a sail,
the cool blue air is like a diamond ring.
In our room the stars pale.
Far off,
          in the depths of the sky's stream, stones wash clean.
On the pillow, my rose is sleeping —
          her head is on the enormous feather pillow.
Her hands on the quilt are like two white tulips.
Birds start singing in her hair.
In the early light, the city with its trees and factory chimneys.
The trees are wet, the chimneys hot.
Caressing the asphalt,
          the first footsteps pass through our room,
              the hum of the first engine,
                  the first laugh,
                  the first curse.
The steam in the glass case of the pastry cart,
the driver in boots going into the dairy store,
the neighbors' crying child,
the dove in the blue poster,
the manikin in the window
              with yellow shoes,
and Chinese fans of sandalwood
and those thick red lips of hers
and the happiest and freshest of all awakenings
              pass through our room in the early light.
I turn on the radio:

metals with giant names mix with giant numbers,
oil wells race with cornfields.
The shepherd who got the Lenin Medal
            (I saw his picture on the front pages,
                his thick mustache black and drooping)
speaks like a young girl, shy and embarrassed.
Then it moves on to the news from both poles:
then as the third sputnik
            circles the earth for the 8878th time
                at six o'clock this morning,
the huge eyes of my rose open on the pillow.
They're still like smoky mountain lakes.
Blue fish flicker in them,
green pines rise in their depths.
They look out deep and flat.
The last of her dreams flashes in the early morning.
I'm illuminated,
I see and know myself once more.
I'm recklessly happy
            and a little bit embarrassed,
                but only a little bit.
In the early morning the light in our room
            is like a sail ready for a voyage,
                a sail of light.
My rose gets out of bed naked like an apricot.
In the early light the bed is pure white
            like the dove in the blue poster.

            February 1960,
            Kislovodsk

POEM

My woman came with me as far as Brest,
she got off the train and stayed on the platform,
she grew smaller and smaller,
she became a kernel of wheat in the infinite blue,
then all I could see were the tracks.
Then, she called out to me from Poland, I couldn't answer,
I couldn't ask, "Where are you my rose, where are you?"
"Come," she said, I couldn't reach her,
the train was going like it would never stop,
I was choking with grief.
Then, patches of snow were rotting on the sandy earth,
then suddenly I knew that my woman was watching,
"Did you forget me," she was asking, "did you forget me?"
as for spring it was marching with muddy bare feet on the sky.
Then, stars lighted on the telegraph wires,
as for darkness it lashed the train like rain,
my woman was standing under the telegraph poles,
her heart was pounding too as if she were in my arms,
the poles kept disappearing she was still there,
the train was going like it would never stop,
I was choking with grief.
Then suddenly I knew I'd been on this train for years and years,
— but I'm still amazed at how or why I knew this —
and always singing the same great hopeful song
I'm forever leaving the cities and women I love
and I'm carrying my losses like a wound opening inside me
and I'm getting closer, I'm getting closer to somewhere.

March 1960,
Mediterranean

POEM

Suddenly something tears inside me and catches in my throat,
suddenly, in the middle of my work, I jump up,
suddenly I see a dream, in a hotel, in the hall, standing up,
suddenly the tree on the sidewalk hits me in the forehead,
suddenly a wolf howls at the moon, unhappy, angry, starved,
suddenly the stars are hanging from a swing in a garden,
suddenly I think how I'll be in the grave,
suddenly in my head there's a sunny haze,
suddenly I cling to the day I began as if it would never end,
and each time you float up to the surface of the water. . .

8 September 1960

POEM

Morning, six o'clock.
I opened the door of the day and stepped in,
the taste of young blue greeted me in the window,
in the mirror the lines on my forehead left over from yesterday,
and behind me a woman's voice softer than peach fuzz
and on the radio news of my country
and now, my greed filling and overflowing,
I'll run from tree to tree in the orchard of the hours
and the sun will set, my dear,
and I hope beyond the night
the taste of a new blue will be waiting for me, I hope.

14 September 1960

STRAW-BLOND

to Vera Tulyakova,
with my deep respect

I

at dawn the express entered the station unannounced
it was covered with snow
I was on the platform my coat collar raised
there was no one on the platform but me
a window of the sleeper stopped in front of me
its curtains were parted
a young woman was sleeping in the lower berth in the twilight
her hair straw-blond eyelashes blue
and her full red lips looked spoiled and pouting
I didn't see who was sleeping in the upper berth
unannounced the express slipped out of the station
I don't know where it came from or where it's going
I watched it leave
I was sleeping in the upper berth
                              in the Bristol Hotel in Warsaw
I hadn't fallen into such deep sleep in years
and yet my bed was wooden and narrow
a young woman was sleeping in another bed
her hair straw-blond eyelashes blue
her white neck was long and smooth
she hadn't fallen into such deep sleep in years
and yet her bed was wooden and narrow
time sped on we were nearing midnight
we hadn't fallen into such deep sleep in years
and yet the beds were wooden and narrow
I'm coming down the stairs from the fourth floor
the elevator is out again
inside mirrors I'm coming down the stairs

I could be twenty I could be a hundred
time sped on we were nearing midnight
on the third floor a woman is laughing behind a door
          a sad rose opens slowly in my right hand
I met a Cuban ballerina at the snowy windows on the second
                                             floor
she flashed past my forehead like a fresh dark flame
the poet Nicolas Guillen went back to Havana long ago
for years we sat in the hotel lobbies of Europe and Asia
          drinking the loss of our cities drop by drop
there are two things forgotten only with death
the face of our mothers and the face of our cities
and wooden barges swim into the wind early mornings in winter
          like old rowboats that have cut themselves loose
and in the ashes of a brazier
          my big Istanbul wakes up from sleep
there are two things forgotten only with death
the doorman saw me off his cloak sinking into the night
I walked into the icy wind and neon
time sped on I was nearing midnight
they came upon me suddenly
it was light as day but no one else saw them
there was a squad of them
they had jackboots pants coats
arms swastikas on their arms
hands automatics in their hands
they had shoulders helmets on their shoulders but no heads
between their shoulders and their helmets nothing
they even had collars and necks but no heads
they were soldiers whose deaths are not mourned
we walked on
you could see their fear animal fear
I can't say it showed in their eyes
they didn't have heads to have eyes
you could see their fear animal fear

it showed in their boots
can boots show fear
theirs did
in their fear they opened fire
they're firing nonstop at all buildings all vehicles all living things
at every sound the least movement
they even fired at a poster with blue fish on Chopin Street
but not so much as a piece of plaster falls or a glass breaks
and no one but me hears the shots
the dead even an SS squad the dead can't kill
the dead kill by coming back by becoming worms and going
                                        inside the apple
but you could see their fear animal fear
wasn't this city killed before they were
weren't the bones of this city broken one by one and its skin
                                        flayed
weren't bookcovers made from its skin soap from its oil rope
                                        from its hair
but here it was standing before them
like a hot loaf of bread in the icy night wind
time sped on I was nearing midnight
on Belvedere road I thought of the Poles
they dance a heroic mazurka through history
on Belvedere road I thought of the Poles
in this palace they gave me my first and maybe last medal
the master of ceremonies opened the gilded white door
I entered the big hall with a young woman
her hair straw-blond eyelashes blue
and no one was there but us two
plus the aquarelles and the delicate chairs and couches like in
                                        doll houses
and you became
                a picture done in light blue or a porcelain doll mayb
or maybe a spark from my dream come down on my chest
you were sleeping in the lower berth in the twilight
your white neck was long and smooth

124

you hadn't fallen into such deep sleep in years
and here the Caprice Bar in Cracow
time speeds on we're nearing midnight
separation was on the table between the coffee cup and my glass
you put it there
it was the water at the bottom of a stone well
I lean over and look
an old man is dimly smiling at a cloud
I call out
the echoes of my voice return losing you
separation was on the table in the cigarette package
the waiter with the glasses brought it but you ordered it
it was smoke curling in your eyes
it was at the tip of your cigarette
and in your hand ready to say goodbye
separation was on the table where you rested your elbow
it was in what went through your mind
        in what you hid from me and what you didn't
separation was in your calm
        in your trust in me
it was in your great fear
to fall in love with someone out of the blue as if your door
                                suddenly opened
actually you love me and don't know it
separation was in your not knowing
separation was free of gravity weightless I can't say like a feather
even a feather has weight separation was weightless but it was
time speeds on midnight is nearing
we walked in the shadow of medieval walls that touched the stars
time was speeding backward
the echoes of our steps returned like scrawny yellow dogs
they were running behind us in front of us
the devil wanders Jagiellonian University
digging his nails into the stones
he's out to sabotage the astrolabe Copernicus got from the Arabs

and in the market place under the Cloth Arcade
he's with the Catholic students dancing to rock 'n' roll
time speeds on we're nearing midnight
the red glow of Nowa Huta strikes the clouds
there young workers from villages cast their souls along with
                                                          metal
burning into new molds
and casting souls is a thousand times harder than casting metal
the trumpet that sounds the hours in the bell tower of the
                                                  Church of St. Mary
rang midnight
its cry rose up from the Middle Ages
            warned of the enemy nearing the city
and was suddenly silenced by the arrow that pierced its throat
the trumpet died at peace
and I thought of the pain
of seeing the enemy approach but being killed before telling
time speeds on midnight recedes
like a boat station just gone dark
at dawn the express entered the station unannounced
Prague was all rain
it was an inlaid-silver chest at the bottom of a lake
I opened it
inside a young woman is sleeping among glass birds
her hair straw-blond eyelashes blue
she hasn't fallen into such deep sleep in years
I closed the chest put it on the baggage car
unannounced the express slipped out of the station
I watched it leave my arms hanging at my sides
Prague was all rain
you aren't here
you're sleeping in the lower berth in the twilight
the upper berth is empty
you aren't here
one of the most beautiful cities in the world is empty
empty like a glove you pulled off your hand

it went dark like mirrors that no longer see you
the waters of the Vltava disappear under bridges like lost nights
the streets are all empty
in all the windows the curtains are closed
the streetcars go by all empty
            they don't even have conductors or drivers
coffeehouses are empty
            bars and restaurants too
store windows are empty
            no cloth no crystal no meat no wine
            not a book not a box of candy not a carnation
and in this loneliness enfolding the city like fog an old man
trying to shake off the sadness of age increased tenfold by
loneliness throws bread to the gulls from Legionnaires Bridge
            dipping each piece in the blood
            of his too-young heart
I want to catch the minutes
the gold dust of their speed stays on my fingers
a woman is sleeping in the lower berth in the sleeper
she hasn't fallen into such deep sleep in years
her hair straw-blond eyelashes blue
her hands candles in silver candlesticks
I couldn't see who was sleeping in the upper berth
if anyone is sleeping there it isn't me
maybe the upper berth is empty
maybe Moscow is in the upper berth
fog's settled over Poland
            over Brest too
for two days now planes can't land or take off
but the trains come and go they go through hollowed-out eyes
since Berlin I've been alone in the compartment
the next morning I woke up to the sun of snowy fields
in the dining car I drank a kind of *ayran* called kefir
the waitress recognized me
she'd seen two of my plays in Moscow
a young woman met me at the station

her waist smaller than an ant's
her hair straw-blond eyelashes blue
I took her hand we walked
we walked in the sun cracking the snow
spring was early that year
those were the days they were flying news to the evening star
Moscow was happy I was happy we were happy
I lost you suddenly in Mayakovsky Square suddenly I lost you
no not suddenly because first I lost the warmth of your hand
in mine then I lost the soft weight of your hand in my palm
and then your hand
and separation had set in long before at the first touch of our
                                                            fingers
but I still lost you suddenly
on the seas of asphalt I stopped the cars and looked inside no
                                                            you
the boulevards are under snow
yours are not among the footprints
I know your footprints in boots shoes stockings bare
I asked the guards
didn't you see
if she took off her gloves you couldn't miss her hands
her hands are candles in silver candlesticks
the guards answer very politely
we didn't see
a tugboat comes through the current at Seraglio Point in
                                                            Istanbul
behind it three barges
awk awk the sea gulls go awk awk
I called out to the barges from Red Square I couldn't call to
the tugboat captain because the way his engine was roaring
he wouldn't have heard me and the captain was tired too and
his coat buttons were all torn off
I called out to the barges from Red Square
we didn't see
I stood I'm standing in all the lines in all the streets of Moscow

and I'm asking only the women
old women quiet and patient with smiling faces under wool
                                                    babushkas
young woman rosy-cheeked and straight-nosed in green velvet
                                                        hats
and young girls very clean and firm and elegant too
maybe there are frightful old women weary young women
                                              and sloppy girls
          but who cares about them
women spot beauty before men do and they don't forget it
didn't you see
her hair straw-blond eyelashes blue
her black coat has a white collar and big pearly buttons
she got it in Prague
we didn't see
I'm racing the minutes now they're ahead now me
when they're ahead I'm scared I'll lose sight
of their disappearing red lights
when I'm ahead their spotlights throw my shadow on the road
my shadow races ahead of me I'm suddenly afraid I'll lose
sight of my shadow
I go into theaters concerts movies
I didn't go to the Bolshoi you don't like the opera playing tonight
I went into Fisherman's Bar in Kalamish in Istanbul and we
sat talking sweetly with Sait Faik I was out of prison a month
his liver was hurting and the world was beautiful
I go into restaurants brassy orchestras the bands of the famous
I ask doormen with gold braid aloof tip-loving waiters
the people in the checkrooms and our neighborhood watchman
we didn't see
the clock tower of the Strastnoi Monastery rang midnight
actually both the tower and the monastery were knocked
                                              down long ago
they're building the biggest movie house of the city there
that's where I met my nineteenth year
we recognized each other right away

yet we hadn't seen each other not even photographs
we still recognized each other right away we weren't surprised
we wanted to shake hands
but our hands couldn't touch forty years of time stood between u
a North Sea frozen and endless
and it started snowing in Strastnoi Square now Pushkin Square
I'm cold especially my hands and feet
yet I have wool socks and fur-lined boots and gloves
he was the one without socks his feet wrapped in cloth in old
boots his hands bare
the world the taste of a green apple in his mouth
the hardness of a fourteen-year-old girl's breast in his hands
songs go for miles and miles in his eyes death measures a hand's-
span
and he knows nothing of what will happen to him
only I know what will happen to him
because I believed in everything that he believed in
I loved all the women he's going to love
I wrote all the poems he's going to write
I sat in all the prisons he'll sit in
I passed through all the cities he'll pass through
I suffered all his illnesses
I slept all his sleeps dreamed all his dreams
I lost all that he will lose
her hair straw-blond eyelashes blue
her black coat has a white collar and huge pearly buttons
I didn't see

II

my nineteenth year passes through Beyazit Square and comes
out on Red Square
goes down to Concorde I meet Abidin and we talk of squares
the day before yesterday Gagarin went around the greatest of
them and came back
Titov too will go around and come back seventeen and a half
times even but I don't know about this yet

we talk of spaces and structures with Abidin in my attic hotel
room
and the Seine flows on both sides of Notre Dame
at night from my window I see the Seine as a slice of the moon
on the wharf of the stars
and a young woman is sleeping in my attic room
mixed with the chimneys of the Paris roofs
she hasn't fallen into such deep sleep in years
her straw-blond hair is curled her blue eyelashes are clouds on
her face
we're talking with Abidin about the space in the seed of the
atom and the structure in the seed of the atom
we talk of Rumi whirling in space
Abidin paints the colors of unlimited speed
I eat up the colors like fruit
and Matisse is a fruitseller he sells the fruits of the cosmos
and so is our Abidin and Avni and Levni
and the structures spaces and colors seen by the microscope
and rocket portholes
and their poets painters and musicians
in the space of one hundred fifty by sixty Abidin paints the
surge forward the way I can see and catch the fish in the water
that's how I can see and catch the sparkling flowing moments
of Abidin's canvas
and the Seine is like a slice of the moon
a young woman sleeps on the slice of the moon
how many times have I lost her how many times have I found
her and how many more times will I lose her and find her
that's the way it is girl that's how it is I dropped part of my life
into the Seine from the St. Michel bridge
the part of my life will catch on Monsieur Dupont's fishline one
morning in drizzling light
Monsieur Dupont will pull it out of the water along with the
blue picture of Paris he won't make anything of the part of
my life it won't be like a fish or a shoe
Monsieur Dupont will throw it back in along with the blue

131

picture of Paris
the picture will stay in its old place
the part of my life will flow with the Seine into the great
cemetery of rivers
I woke up to the rustle of the blood flowing in my veins
my fingers are weightless
my fingers and toes are going to break off take to the air and
circle lazily over my head
I don't have a right or a left an up or a down
I should tell Abidin to paint the one martyred in Beyazit
Square and comrade Gagarin and comrade Titov whose
name or fame or face I don't know yet and those to come
after him and the young woman sleeping in the attic
I got back from Cuba this morning
in the space that is Cuba six million people whites blacks
yellows mulattoes are planting a bright seed the seed of seeds
joyously
can you paint happiness Abidin
but without taking the easy way out
not the picture of the angel-faced mother nursing her rosy-
cheeked baby
nor the apples on white cloth
nor the goldfish darting among the bubbles in the aquarium
can you paint happiness Abidin
can you paint Cuba in midsummer 1961
master can you paint Praise be praise be I saw the day I could
die now and not be sorry
can you paint What a pity what a pity we could have been
born in Havana this morning
I saw a hand 150 kilometers east of Havana close to the sea
I saw a hand on a wall
the wall was an open song
the hand caressed the wall
the hand was six months old and was stroking its mother's neck
the hand was seventeen years old and caressed Maria's breasts
its palm was calloused and smelled of the Caribbean

it was twenty years old and stroked the neck of its six-
                                    month-old son
the hand was twenty-five years old and had forgotten how to
                                    caress
the hand was thirty years old and I saw it on a wall by the
    sea 150 kilometers east of Havana it was caressing the
                                    wall
Abidin you draw hands the hands of our laborers and iron-
    workers draw in charcoal the hand of the Cuban
                        fisherman Nicolas too
the hand of the Cuban fisherman Nicolas who on the wall of
    the shiny house he got from the cooperative rediscovered
                        caressing and will never lose it again
a big hand
a sea turtle of a hand
a hand that doesn't believe it can caress an open wall
a hand that now believes in all joys
a sunny salty sacred hand
the hand of hopes that sprout green and sweeten with the
speed of sugar cane in earth as fertile as the words of Fidel
one of the hands in Cuba in 1961 that plant houses like very
    colorful cool trees and trees like very comfortable houses
one of the hands getting ready to pour steel
the hand that makes songs of machine guns and machine guns
                                    of songs
the hand of freedom without lies
the hand Fidel shook
the hand that writes the word freedom with the first pencil
                        of its life on the first paper of its life
when they say the word freedom the Cubans' mouths water
as if they were cutting into a honey of a melon
and the men's eyes shine
and the girls melt when their lips touch the word freedom
and the old people draw from the well their sweetest memories
                                    and slowly sip them
can you paint happiness Abidin
can you paint the word freedom the kind without lies

night is falling in Paris
Notre Dame lit up like an orange lamp and went out
and in Paris all the stones old and new lit up like an orange
lamp and went out
I think of our crafts the business of poetry pictures music-
making and so on
I think and I understand
that a grand river flows since the time the first human hand
drew the first bison in the first cave
then all streams run into it with their new fish new water
grasses new tastes and it alone flows endlessly and
never dries up
there's supposed to be a chestnut tree in Paris
the first of the Paris chestnuts the ancestor of all chestnuts
in Paris
it came from Istanbul and settled in Paris from the hills of
the Bosporus
I don't know if it's still alive it would be about two hundred
years old
I wished I could go kiss its hand
I wished we could go lie in its shade the people who make the
paper for this book who set its type who print its drawings
the people who sell this book in their stores who pay money
and buy it who buy it and look at it and Abidin and me too
plus the straw-blond trouble of my life

1961, Train, Warsaw, Cracow, Prague,
Moscow, Paris, Havana, Moscow

BERLIN LETTERS

1.

Berlin is bright and sunny.
March 8, 1963.
Happy holidays, my woman.
I forgot to say it on the phone this morning.
When I hear your voice I forget the world.
Many happy returns, my beauty.

8 March 1963

2.

In four days I'll be in Moscow.
This separation too will end, thank God, and I'll return.
This separation too will be left behind like a rainy road.
New separations will come,
I'll descend into new wells,
I'll go somewhere and come back.
I'll run, breathless, to new returns.
Then neither Berlin nor Tanganyika —
nowhere, I'll go nowhere.
I won't be able to return — no boat, no train, no plane.
No letters will come from me, and no telegrams.
And I won't be able to call you on the phone.
You won't laugh softly at my voice.
And you won't get any news from me either,
you'll be left all by yourself.
In four days I'll be in Moscow.
Berlin is bright and sunny.
It's spring in Moscow,
you said so on the phone.
This separation too will end, thank God, and I'll return.
But inside me is the night of our great separation,

inside me the pain of your being without me,
inside me your loneliness.
Loneliness: the bread of memories that doesn't satisfy,
    the call of memories to distance: loneliness.
Maybe three months, maybe three years,
loneliness will be your shadow.
In four days I'll be in Moscow.
It's spring in Moscow,
you said so on the phone.

8 April 1963

3.
In five hours I'll be at your side.
In my hotel room in Berlin, sunlight,
        moist bird chirpings
            — it rained this morning —
                and streetcars too
                    and time.
Time just doesn't flow,
it's frozen solid.
You can hang it on a hanger,
you can cut it with a knife.
It's as if I'm in prison.
In prison the cruelest guard
            is time.
In two hours I'll be at the airport.
In five hours in your blue.
In five hours, freedom.
In the hotel rooms of all returns
they should put up a statue of whoever invented the airplane.

12 April 1963

MY FUNERAL

Will my funeral start out from our courtyard?
How will you take me down from the third floor?
The coffin won't fit in the elevator,
and the stairs are awfully narrow.

Maybe the sun will be knee-deep in the courtyard, and there'll
                                                    be pigeons,
maybe there will be snow full of the shouts of children,
maybe rain with its wet asphalt.
And the garbage cans will stand in the courtyard as always.

If, as is the custom here, I'm put on the truck face open,
something might drop on my forehead from a pigeon: it's
                                                    good luck.
Whether there's a band or not, the children will come up to me,
children are curious about the dead.

Our kitchen window will watch me leave.
Our balcony will see me off with the wash on the line.
In this yard I was happier than you'll ever know.
Neighbors, I wish you all long lives.

April 1963, Moscow

NOTES

Page 19: ON SHIRTS, TROUSERS, CAPS, AND FELT HATS: This poem is Hikmet's answer to those members of the literary establishment who not only attacked his poetry but ridiculed him for affecting "proletarian" dress; "Sat-Sin" is a made-up name that probably refers to one of these critics.

Page 26: THE EPIC OF SHEIK BEDREDDIN: Sheik Bedreddin was born in Simavne in the province of Edirne sometime between 1359 and 1365 and studied in Edirne, Konya, and Cairo. He returned to Edirne as a high-level judge under Prince Musa, but when Musa was murdered by his brother Mehmet, Bedreddin was exiled to Iznik. There he began preaching revolution and eventually fled to Dobruja, where he organized a rebellion against Sultan Mehmet I. He was captured, tried, and executed in Serrai in 1420.

Ducas (1400-71), Byzantine historian who wrote an important history of the rise of the Ottomans.

Börklüje Mustafa, a Turkish peasant from Karaburun, spread Bedreddin's ideas in the provinces of Izmir and Aydin. He succeeded in uniting the diverse population of the region in uprisings against two regional governors but ultimately was defeated by Sultan Mehmet's army. Taken to Seljuk and tortured, he was crucified in 1417.

Arabshah (1389-1450), Arabic scholar and poet.

Ashikpashazade (b. 1400), Ottoman historian.

Neshri, fifteenth-century Ottoman historian.

Idris of Bitlis (d. 1520), Ottoman statesman and historian who wrote a verse-history of the reigns of the first eight Ottoman sultans called *Eight Heavens.*

Prince Musa ascended the throne in Edirne in 1411 but was killed by his brother Mehmet in 1413.

Sultan Mehmet I, who ruled from 1412 until his death in 1421, unified the Ottoman Empire after numerous wars with his brothers.

Prince Murad (1404-51), son of Sultan Mehmet I, led the Sultan's army against Börklüje Mustafa in 1416 and, in 1421, became Sultan Murad II.

Bayezid Pasha (d. 1421), Sultan Mehmet's vizier and commander of the army sent against Börklüje Mustafa.

Torlak Kemal, a Jew who preached Bedreddin's philosophy in the province of Manisa and led the revolt there, was captured and killed by Bayezid Pasha in 1417.

Mevlana Haydar, Persian scholar reported — perhaps wrongly — to have pronounced the death sentence on Bedreddin.

Shekerullah bin Shehabeddin, Ottoman historian.

Page 61: LETTERS FROM CHANKIRI PRISON, 2: Ghazali (d. 1534), Ottoman poet from Bursa.
Pirayé, Hikmet's second wife.

Page 68: LETTER TO KEMAL TAHIR: Kemal Tahir, the contemporary Turkish writer, who was in prison during the same years (1938-50) as Hikmet.

Page 91: ON IBRAHIM BALABAN'S "SPRING PICTURE": Ibrahim Balaban, Turkish painter who was in prison with Hikmet.

Page 112: I GOT A LETTER FROM MÜNEVVER SAYING: Münevver Andaç was Hikmet's third wife; the Turkish government kept her from joining him in exile. Educated in France and now living in Paris, she has translated many of his works into French.

Page 113: I WROTE A LETTER TO MÜNEVVER SAYING: Memet is Hikmet's son, born in 1950.

Page 122: STRAW-BLOND, I: Vera Tulyakova, the young woman Hikmet lived with during the last years of his life.

Sait Faik (1906-54), Turkish novelist and short-story writer.

II: Abidin Dino, Turkish artist who has illustrated some of Hikmet's books.

Rumi (1207-73), Persian mystic poet who lived in Turkey and founded in Konya the order of whirling dervishes.

Avni Arbaş, Turkish painter living in Paris.

Levni (d. 1732), Ottoman painter of minatures.